WIFI KIDS & ANALOGUE PARENTS

Raising Disciplined and Well Rounded Children in This Digital Age

WIFI KIDS & ANALOGUE PARENTS

Raising Disciplined and Well Rounded Children in This Digital Age

TEMI OLAJIDE

Published by: Proficia Books

Email: proficiabooks@yahoo.com

First Published 2019

ISBN: 978-978-946-489-0

Dedication

To my dear husband and beautiful children:
For being part of this journey, for your constant encouragement, support and prayers. This book wouldn't have been a reality without you all.

To my mum, my number one cheerleader, coach and teacher of life:
For being an exemplary role model.

To my late father, Rev. Timothy Kolade:
For being my hero and my number one mentor. Your death drove me to my purpose and taught me the principles of dying empty.

Acknowledgements

I want to appreciate Moyofade Ipadeola, Mofoluwaso Ilevbare, Steve Harris, Tricia Ikponmwonba, Seun Ilevbare, Kemi Ademiju and my team, for your support during this process of bringing my dream to life.

A big shout out to my brothers, family and friends for being part of my analogue and WiFi journey.

To my Mummyclinicc Tribe, thank you for trusting me with your parenting journey, this book wouldn't have been possible without you all. You mamas rock!

A big thanks to my pastor, Rev. Boladale, for speaking this book to life. Your words to me that day; "You need to write a book on parenting in this digital age," has become a reality today.

Thank you. Love you all!

Contents

Dedication   i

Acknowledgements   iii

Foreword   vii

Introduction   xi

CHAPTER ONE:
OLD PEEPS, NEW PEEPS!   1

CHAPTER TWO:
GO DIGITAL OR GET KICKED OUT!   21

CHAPTER THREE:
LET'S HAVE A CLEARER VIEW!   37

CHAPTER FOUR:
ARE YOU STEPPING UP YOUR GAME?   55

CHAPTER FIVE:

DON'T UNDERESTIMATE THE

POWER OF EFFECTIVE COMMUNICATION — 65

CHAPTER SIX:

WHERE ARE THE BOUNDARIES? — 81

CHAPTER SEVEN:

CREATING AND MAINTAINING

EFFECTIVE SLEEP PATTERNS — 93

CHAPTER EIGHT:

LET'S TALK ABOUT SEX! — 109

CHAPTER NINE:

SHOW THE TALK! — 121

EPILOGUE:

BRIDGING THE GAP — 133

REFERENCES — 137

Foreword

t takes a global village to raise a child.

When I became a parent, three things became clear to me. Fact 1: I need to appreciate my parents more - they did such a good job with me. Fact 2: Parenting is a daily process. Fact 3: Raising disciplined and well-rounded kids doesn't just happen. You must be intentional.

Every year, our kids grow faster in curiosity, knowledge, and the audacity to dream, much more than we can imagine. In this book, the author, Temi Olajide, lays bare all our insecurities as parents, questioning our belief systems, behaviors, and challenging our motives in parenting.

The digital age is here to stay and parents must become more intentional about leveraging it. You can't stay ignorant or refuse to adapt; that's a recipe for becoming extinct. You also can't act nonchalantly and allow external influencers raise your children and rule your home. There are pros and cons to digital literacy, social media and trends. The more aware you are about both sides of the coin, the more prepared you would be to harness the benefits and creativity, avoid the pitfalls, and raise the next generation of confident children, positive social change activists, risk takers, inventors, and more.

Do you have parenting goals? The hallmark of meeting those goals is your level of personal growth and development. Growth comes from learning, unlearning, and relearning something new every day. Your personal growth in all things digital enhances your leadership ability as a parent/guardian and helps you communicate effectively with the kids entrusted in your care. Make a commitment to be actively involved in their lives and transfer good values that will outlive you.

As parents, we have a responsibility to partner with God everyday to bring out the best we can in our children, teaching them great values, helping them solve knotty questions as best as we can, and where we can't, acknowledge it and ask for professional help. Our joy is that they turn out to be positive role models in society, and this cultivating process starts long before they are born.

If you want to know how to communicate effectively with your kids, how to create healthy boundaries around digital content, or if you feel uncomfortable handling your children's sex education, this is your go-to guide.

A big thanks to Temi, the MummyClinicc Coach and Nigeria's #1 Sleep Consultant, for awakening our curiosity, expanding our knowledge, challenging our attitude, and providing practical life tips in this book. This is truly a "must-read" for every modern parent, guardian and teacher.

Mofoluwaso Ilevbare

Author. Speaker. Life Balance Coach

x

Introduction

Like it or not, the world has changed! Gone are the days of analogue phones and VHS players. We're in the age of super-smartphones and online TV. The technological evolution we're experiencing now is mind-blowing. The possibilities are boundless. The things we saw as science fiction while we were growing up are now an everyday occurrence.

Who would have thought a day would come when we would carry so many devices in our pockets and bags? Have I lost you? Okay, let me be clearer. The smartphone you put in your bag and/or pocket is actually many devices in one. Just think of the numerous devices you have on that phone; phone, radio/record player, video player, computer, camera, video recorder, voice recorder, calendar, calculator, Bible/Quran, address book, album, clock, notepad, folders, etc. Wow, right? Not yet! Now think of the institutions and organizations you carry in that same phone – bank, post office, library, market, conference rooms, etc. So, you see, it's a different world from the one we grew up in. Now, that is just one aspect of the digital world; it is so vast and hydra-headed. This is the world our children are born into.

Because the world has changed, people have changed, institutions have changed, relationships have changed, education has changed, businesses have changed, the general outlook to life has changed. You know what else needs to change, and urgently too? Parenting! It's amazing how we have changed in every way except in the ways we raise our children.

A lot of parents raise their children the way they were raised, forgetting that they were raised in the analogue era, while their children are being raised in the digital age. It's a different ball game and like everything else, the dynamics of parenting has to change.

The digital era is a world of possibilities and discoveries, no doubt. However, it also comes with a lot of baggage, especially for parents. It exposes our children to numerous dangers which weren't available when we were growing up, at least not in such proportions. How can we then raise disciplined and well-rounded children in this digital age?

My experience as a parent born in the analogue era as well as my encounters with clients and fellow parents who're also analogue alumni, birthed this book. It became apparent to me that except there is a paradigm shift in the way we parent in this digital age, there's going to be a lot of casualties in the nearest future.

I hope this book helps you make that shift.

Temi Olajide

2019

CHAPTER ONE

OLD PEEPS, NEW PEEPS!

Hello Wet Dream…

On a beautiful Saturday evening, I got the shocker of my life! I was folding our fresh laundry when my ten-year-old son popped a question that made me freeze. "Mum, what is a wet dream?" Oh my goodness! What did I just hear from my baby? When did I give birth to him? Good heavens, was I destabilized? You bet! I quickly regained my composure as the smart mum that I am. I calmly explained to him as much as I could, trying very hard to keep a straight face and mask the butterflies in my stomach. He kept on asking questions and I kept answering to the best of my ability. As you would expect, my answers birthed more questions. Eventually, the session ended. I sat down on the bed, drained. I made a quick mental note to have a serious discussion with his dad. He needs to start that man to man talk immediately. My son's line of questions made me realize he'd been having this discussion with his friends. Your guess is right; I didn't let his dad settle in properly in the evening before giving him the bombshell. He was as taken aback as I was. "They teach them these things too early in school these days, which is wrong. I didn't learn these things until I was like fourteen," he said. "This is not a biology issue o," I told him. "He's clearly been talking with the boys. We need to give him superior knowledge before he starts internalizing what he hears outside." My husband agreed and promised to talk to him.

-Moyofade

Minister for Defence

"She's right, mum!" That was Hammed, my first son. Hammed is nine years old. I was giving his seven-year-old sister, Aishat, certain instructions and she told me she had an objection. Objection? Did I hear right? Objection to what I was instructing? When did that start? As I was about giving her the full treatment, her brother came to her defence, telling me his sister was right. Is this a joke? My own children are now raising objections to my instructions? What exactly is this world turning into? "Children should be allowed to express themselves." That was Hammed again. This time, I pulled the brakes and parked the car. I needed to know what exactly is going on with my children. "In some of our favorite cartoons on TV, they always tell us that children should not be shut up, that we should be allowed to speak out. It's called assertiveness," Hammed further educated me. By this time, I was boiling with anger. "You know what else is called assertiveness? My right to stop you from ever watching TV in that house! I'm stopping all subscription!" I yelled. What effrontery!

-Memunat

He's a fast learner!

A while ago, I went to visit my friend and his family. I carried their three-year-old, Sam, and was playing with him when he suddenly started saying, "Pack you". Before I could try and translate what that meant, his mother smiled and came to the rescue. "He's saying, 'F*ck you'. He hears it from the movies we watch. He's such a fast learner, isn't he?" Wow! To say I was dumbfounded is an understatement. How do I even start disabusing the poor child's mind?

-Edet

Unbelievable! My Baby Knows Where Babies Come From...

It was a Sunday afternoon after church, and after lunch, we were lounging in the living room as usual. My husband had to leave me and my daughter to go and receive a call. I had a light bulb moment and asked my eight-year-old princess where babies come from. To my utmost shock, she gave a step-by-step lecture of sexual intercourse. By the time she was through, I had to pinch myself to be sure it was not a dream. I could have sworn she thought babies dropped from heaven. This was a girl whose privates we still called by a pet name. Can you believe she called 'veejay' by its real name? When she finished, she gave me that smile that says, "You must really think I believe those cock and bull stories you tell me." I had to quickly rush to the rest room to regain my composure. What! Who told her all these things? Until I turned sixteen, I thought I would get pregnant if a man touched me with his hands because that was what my mother told me. I fled anytime a man came close to me because I didn't want to 'catch' pregnancy. So, you must imagine my shock when my eight-year-old daughter told me certain things I didn't know until late in my teens.

-Chinwe

Did your parents deny you access?

"Mum, my tablet can't see the WIFI. What's wrong with the network?" That was Yemi, my five-year-old boy. "Nothing is wrong with the network, Darling. I removed your tablet from WIFI connection," I said. "Why mum?" he asked, his face clouding. "Nothing, I just feel you're too young to have unrestricted access to the internet." You needed to have seen my son's face. "Mum, why are you doing this to me? That was how you changed the password of your phone and I couldn't browse with it again. That was also how you said I couldn't watch the TV and play games all day. Why not? I'm a boy, not a man. Can't I play again? Did your parents do this to you? Did they stop you from using their phones? Did they stop you from watching TV and playing games as long as you wanted?" Yemi went on and on and I just kept looking at him. I was dumfounded! When did access to the internet become a child's right? Did we have phones, cable TV or internet in our time?

How do I begin to tell him that our analogue phone was always locked so we wouldn't have access to it? How do I explain that as children, we were never allowed to make calls, we only received calls? How do I tell him TV stations didn't start broadcast until 4pm and closed at 10pm after Network News? How do I, How do I…

-Sade

They Have Feelings Too?

My friend, Ego, called me yesterday. We spoke for about one hour and I stood at the same spot for another one hour after the call, stunned! She had gone to a ten-year-old's birthday party with her four-year-old daughter, Precious. The celebrant was a girl who had a five-year-old brother, Jude. As they were all having fun; children playing in the garden and parents in the house sharing gist, she noticed she couldn't see Precious running around with the other kids. She went out to look for her and behold, she was nowhere to be found. She went back to tell her host and a frantic search began. They eventually found Precious and Jude under the sheets, in Jude's room, kissing mouth to mouth. Ego was shocked beyond words. It was Jude's mum who screamed and asked them what they were doing. Jude said they were playing mummy and daddy game and that he loves Precious. He said it with such deep emotions and it was apparent he'd been watching adult movies. The search group dispersed but Ego has not recovered as I speak. She didn't even know how to handle the situation because she felt like a culprit. She had always playfully called Jude Precious' husband. How could she have known the boy took it so seriously and had really started having feelings for her little Precious? She felt like she had set her own daughter up.

-Nse

Speechless Dad!

"Dad, is Uncle Joe gay?" That was my nine-year-old daughter. I jerked involuntarily and spewed my Fanta on the sofa. "Angel, what did you just say?" I managed to spew, so sure I must have heard wrongly. "I said is Uncle Joe gay?" she repeated, her eyes widening. Oh my goodness! Now, I'm sure. "Gay? What's gay?" I said blankly. I didn't know what else to say. I couldn't even begin to think she knew what gay meant; she had to be referring to the original meaning of gay, right?

"Dad? Gay as in gay, as in fag, as in homosexual?" she explained with that look your professor gives you when he or she thinks you're too dumb. By this time, I had sat straight and put my drink on a stool; this was no time to drink Fanta. I couldn't hide my shock any longer. "A-a-ngel, what do-do you know a-a-bout being g-gay?" I stammered, my voice threatening to fail me. "Dad, I'm nine! Everyone in this world knows what being gay means. I even have friends who said being straight is boring." I'm sure that by this time, my BP must have reached the highest ever. But would you blame me? When you thought you had covered the basics of sex education and your daughter springs this on you, what are you expected to do? Where do I even begin?

-Jeff

God Bless the Slippers Generation

"Chinedu, kneel down there," I said. He had been so troublesome today. "Why, mum?" he asked. What! Six-year-old Chinedu is asking me why I am punishing him? Chai! I have suffered! God bless my mum wherever she is now. If I had ever tried uttering such rubbish even as a teenager, she would have reset my brain with her slippers. What has the world turned into? I cannot punish my own child without being questioned? It took all my willpower not to give him a dirty slap and tell him, "Y ko, Z ni."

-Ngozi

I'm sure I'm not the only one laughing right now. Like it or not, the generation gap has never been more glaring. No matter how trendy or techie you consider yourself to be, our generation is different from our children's. And, trust me, it's one hell of a difference! It's an oldie versus newbie thingy, and the earlier we start making the necessary adjustments so as to raise well-rounded children, the better. Now, what do these true life experiences tell us? Let's briefly analyze the various issues that cropped up in the stories above.

Exposure:

In Ofcom's Media Use and Attitudes report, 2018, there were some very interesting findings. One, they found out that TV and tablets dominate device use of our children. Two, they discovered that half of children between ages 5-15 watch OTT (over the top) television services like Netflix, Amazon Prime Video and Now TV. Three, YouTube is becoming the viewing platform of choice, with rising popularity particularly among 8-11-year-olds. Within this, vloggers are an increasingly important source of content and creativity. Four, online gaming is increasingly popular; three-quarters of 5-15-year-olds who play games do so online.

A 2014 study from New Zealand shows that 88% of 6-14-year-olds live in a home with a computer or laptop, nearly three-quarters of homes had at least one tablet, two-thirds had a games console and half the children had access to a smartphone they could use (New Zealand On Air & Broadcasting Standards Authority, 2015).

Let me ask you how many of these media you had access to while growing up? None? I thought so! If you grew up in a typical urban African home like mine, television stations didn't start broadcast until 4pm. And they produced heavily censored children's programs. The programming was very controlled, so we relied mainly on our peers to get information our parents wouldn't give us. Now, the game has changed tremendously. Our own children are now exposed to myriad information, entertainment, education and opinions. They're even more informed about certain things than we are.

What does this imply? One, they see the world differently. As children, we saw the world as the walls of our homes, schools and religious houses. Now, the world has no enclosure. Not only do our children have access to people anywhere in the world, people all over the world also have access to them. Scary, isn't it? Yes, I know, and as if that is not enough, technology is evolving daily to ensure increased accessibility. Two, they have access to information that is beyond their age-grade literally at the tip of their fingers. So, unlike we, who had our information diet controlled by our parents, relatives, neighbors, teachers and religious leaders, they have an ocean of information unleashed at them. Three, they're more likely to question certain norms because they are exposed to other standards in the media. That, definitely, was not the case while we were growing up.

Audacity/Assertiveness:

The western world is very particular about assertiveness and it is incorporated into their education system. However, we have issues with that as Africans. It isn't embedded in our culture, especially for children. Many of us never dared stare in our parents' eyes, talk more of giving a contrary opinion. Even till now, it's still entrenched in us. We rarely oppose our parents' wishes. This is not the case with our children's generation. They see how their counterparts in the western world address their parents, they see their body language and their liberal outlook on life and they don't see why they should conduct themselves differently. So, you see, that's a huge generational gap there. To us, it's a culture shock, to our children, it's a norm.

Early Maturity:

We need to know that there is a decrease in the age of puberty. Puberty is the phase of life in which physiological changes in the body occur as a result of hormone changes. Girls start puberty sooner than boys, but usually by the mid-teenage years, everyone is experiencing the physical transition to adulthood. Nowadays, there is a rise in precocious maturity, where a child develops earlier than normal. According to Chapa, H., a clinical assistant professor of obstetrics and gynecology at the Texas A&M College of Medicine, "The age of puberty, especially female puberty, has been decreasing in western cultures for decades now. For example, at the turn of the 20th century, the average age for an American girl to get her period was 16 or 17. Today, that number has decreased to 12 or 13 years."

Also, a study from the American Academy of Pediatrics (as stated by A&M University Health Science Center) found that boys were starting puberty earlier than previously recorded. According to the findings, boys are now beginning puberty around, or a little before age 10. Previously, 11 years was the age boys began puberty. The study claimed that the public health implication of these findings is unknown and requires further studies.

What does the above information spell for us as parents? It means our children will require the sex education we had as sixteen- or seventeen-year-olds (if we had any) at age nine or ten. Failure to do so will leave them at the mercy of a barrage of information online and offline.

Inquisitiveness:
Almost all children today are inquisitive. They want to know more. Definitely, we weren't this inquisitive in our days. One major reason was because life wasn't this liberal and there was a limit to what you could ask your parents even if you were confused. The fear of being misunderstood and labeled as

wayward, or worse, beaten blue-black, kept us ignorant. I remember a childhood friend who asked her mother what menstruation was and was scolded and shouted down. She further received a stern lecture on how her life would be totally ruined if she as much as spoke to a boy or man, complete with examples of women whose lives had been 'ruined' because they messed around with men. Note that her question was never answered. Would one expect a girl like that to ask any more questions? Of course not! Her inquisitiveness had been quenched, perhaps forever. A good number of us scampered for safety at the hoot of our fathers' cars and there was never family time where children could voice their opinions. In fact, wasn't there a saying that, "Children are to be seen, not heard"? Our children have it very differently. They are encouraged to open up to us and ask questions. Also, education has evolved and being curious is now an advantage. But how prepared are we for the curiosity level of our children? Remember, we have no templates from our parents to look at; therefore, we need to develop our own roadmap.

Whether we like it or not, the world has evolved. When we were growing up, the analogue telephone was found in very few homes and businesses. It was the exclusive preserve of the elite. It was a luxury and symbol status. Now, practically everyone, kids inclusive, has a phone or access to one. In our days, if you had a Peugeot 504/505 or Volks Wagen Beatle, you were considered well to do. These cars are now museum items. The VHS player was owned only by the rich and neighbors often gathered at their windows to get a glimpse of the latest movies. Now, with a smartphone, you have access to limitless movies, right on your palm. Our children have never seen a VHS player before. In those days, we played physical games like ludo, snakes and ladders, monopoly, etc., nowadays digital games are the in-thing. In our time, we played outdoors more often, we had a lot of outdoor games; we were allowed to get fresh air and play with sand. Now, with the advent of smartphones and cable TV, our children spend more time indoors than outdoors.

We now have a lot of time and energy saving devices and technology; washing machine, dish washer, microwave and online food hubs. In our days, we did our chores manually. We washed our own clothes and our parents' clothes, we ironed, washed plates, rotated cooking, swept the premises, cut the grass, etc. Our parents saw it as a form of home training and it has helped us to be the independent, hardworking and productive people we are today. Our children, on the other hand, do little or no house chores; there is one device or a maid, cook, nanny, housekeeper, washman or woman, houseboy or gardener to the rescue.

While growing up, we had friendly neighbors. Our parents allowed us stay at neighbor's houses. Our neighbors could correct us and vice versa. Life was safer and there was a considerable level of trust in society. Nowadays, everyone is a suspect, especially your new neighbor who looks like a pervert. You dare not allow your child stay a minute out of your watch, lest you risk endangering the poor child in the hands of molesters.

Back in the day, our parents knew most, if not all of our friends. They could easily tell which friend was good for us and which wasn't. Now, our kids can have numerous 'friends' from all over the world that we would never be aware of.

What about schooling? Quite a number of us used the local black slates and black boards at the outset of our school days. Our children now use all sorts of sophisticated boards, projectors and flat screen TVs. The curriculum then was basic, though encompassing. We had minimal homework which allowed us enough play time. Now, the curriculum is so complex and advanced and our three-year-olds are given science projects as assignments. Many of us didn't start school until we were six years old. Remember how you had to do the test of reaching your ear with the hand on the other side as a way of judging whether you were mature enough to start school? The funnier part of this exercise was that if you were small statured and your hand could not reach your ear; you were disqualified and told to try again the following school year and you would keep trying until you passed the 'litmus' test. But what is obtainable now? Our children start school at three months old, sometimes younger, because mummy's maternity leave is over.

Talking about motherhood, many of our mothers stayed home to raise kids in those days and had more time to take care of their kids and monitor them. Those who worked either had stalls they could take their children to or had teaching and civil service jobs that enabled them close early to be with the kids. Now, with female empowerment and emancipation, women take more challenging and time-consuming jobs that demand they spent increasingly more time out of the home. As a result, children are left at the mercy of teachers and nannies/maids.

Let's talk about food. Then, we had our meals mostly cooked from scratch. We had gardens where we planted vegetables and fruits. Some of us had domestic animals like goats, hens, ducks, turkeys, etc., that served as protein. We ate straight from nature. Now almost everything is processed. We are in the jet age and everyone is in a rush. Any product, service or device that can save time and energy is immediately embraced. So, our children are used to things been done through 'express'. What is the result of this? They are impatient and always looking for shortcuts.

See? It's not the same world in many ramifications. The world has changed and we have to change too if we don't want to be left behind. We cannot raise our 'digital children' with our analogue background and mindset. We need to update and keep updating. Take the phone evolution for example. When handsets came, we were very happy to just have a phone to hold and call ours. Remember the popular Nokia 3310? Some people committed crimes just to own that phone. Now, it's outdated because it wasn't upgraded. The brand was so comfortable with the status quo and its success story that it failed to notice that the world has moved on. Apple, on the other hand, keeps upgrading and keeping up with the trends. Scratch that – it keeps dictating the trend! As a parent, do you want to be like Nokia or do you want to be like Apple? Your choice!

CHAPTER TWO

GO DIGITAL OR GET KICKED OUT!

The Smart Photographer…

We were about moving to a new apartment and I told Bims, my nine-year-old daughter, to write down the names of all the DVDs before packing them so we wouldn't lose any and so that we would be able to take stock in our new home. A week later, after relocating and while arranging the living room, I asked for the list so I could check and be sure we didn't lose any of the DVDs. My daughter came back and handed me my phone. I was about scolding her for being absent-minded when she showed me a picture of the DVDs as arranged in our previous house. OMG! Instead of writing the names of each DVD, my daughter simply snapped them with my phone and that saved her time and energy. I definitely would never have thought of snapping the DVDs. That was a great display of initiative. I've never been prouder as a father.

-Abdullai

Welcome, analogue parent. You know, it struck me the other day that a lot of us went to computer schools at the advent of the computer age. We all would line up behind the proprietor like fashion apprentices to catch a glimpse of the only computer in the 'computer school'. Where on earth did they all disappear to, by the way? How many of our children now go to computer schools? My children would laugh to bits at the thought of a computer school. We paid to go and meet computer but computer came to meet them at the house (in different sleek and portable forms!). The best part is they don't need to be taught, it's a DIY world! And I'm sure you know your six-year-old can navigate your phone better than you. My own son can pass for a computer instructor any day! Today, our children don't have to go to computer schools; they go to coding and programming schools. And guess what? They don't have to gather in a crowded room like we did, they can do it online, from the comfort of their rooms.

This, here, is the digital world and only the digitally savvy can survive. Did I scare you? Don't be scared! It's not as daunting as it sounds. We analogue parents can become digital parents. Let's put aside the fact that we want to raise great kids, don't we also want to excel in this digital world? Of course! So, we need to be up to speed on certain digital advancements. Let's take a quick peek at some of these inventions. And if you're already up to date, let's play catch up!

Google

Now, you can quit playing god with your children. We grew up thinking our parents knew everything; they were the deities of knowledge and wisdom. Now, our children bypass us and consult Google, it's the digital oracle! You're asking why? Because you will also ask Google, so what's the point? Next to our parents were the dictionary, encyclopedia and newspapers, which were our own Google then. Our parents made us read them so we would be knowledgeable. Now, everything our children need is at the touch of a button or screen. It takes a whole lot of stress off us but also introduces a different kind of stress. More on that later! Google has to be the most popular app. There perhaps isn't any modern person who doesn't know about Google. Pray, when was the last time you saw an encyclopedia?

YouTube

Created in 2005, YouTube is a video sharing service where users can create their own profile, upload videos, watch, like and comment on other videos. Millions of users around the world have created accounts on the site that allow them to upload videos that anyone can watch. It is the third most visited website in the world and currently has 15 billion visitors per month. YouTube is the second largest search engine after Google. Over 5 billion hours of video are viewed on YouTube every day.

This translates to over 300 hours of video watched every day. It has been predicted that around half of all under-30s will not pay for a TV subscription because of YouTube (engadget.com). Do you know that more video content is uploaded to YouTube in a 60-day period than the three major U.S. television networks created in 60 years? Also, 70 percent of videos are viewed on mobile devices (mashable.com). Many people now make their living through their YouTube channels; this is made possible through ads, sponsored videos and endorsements. See how this would influence our children's career choices as opposed to the doctor/lawyer options we grew up with? Can you see just how powerful this digital invention is? Now compare it to our 'tales by moonlight' diet? See the difference? Hol'on! We're just getting this party started.

Social Media

This generation has given a whole new meaning to the word 'social'. When we were growing up, being social meant being relatable and perhaps, being at par with trends. The most social of us was made the social prefect in school. That person was the epitome of 'social'. Now, being social without being digital makes absolutely no sense. How else do you catch up on 'gist' from around the world? How do you know how successful your schoolmates have become? How do you advertise your goods and services? How do you keep up with the latest fashion in town? How do you know your dream company is hiring? How do you become aware of new skills you can acquire to develop yourself? How do you know your debtor has just bought a new car? How do you show off your party clothes and beautiful interiors? How do you monitor your spouse's online activities (winks)? And the craze for followership? Let's not even go there. See, social media has not only redefined the word 'social', it has redefined our whole lives. Ignore it at your own peril. So, what exactly is social media and what does it comprise?

Social media refers to websites and applications that are designed to allow people share content quickly, efficiently, and in real-time. This ability to share photos, opinions, events, etc., in real-time has transformed the way we live, the way we view life, the way we do business and most importantly, the way we raise kids. We'll get back to this; let's quickly touch on some social media applications.

Facebook

This is easily the largest social networking site in the world and one of the most widely used. Facebook was perhaps the first that surpassed the landmark of 1 billion user accounts. Apart from the ability to network with friends and relatives, you can also sell on the app and you can even market or promote your business, brand and products by using paid Facebook ads. Facebook is also the place for 'pepper-dem-gangs'. If you need to show off that figure eight you just got, Facebook is the place for you. If you need your enemies to know you have arrived, head straight to Facebook, you'll be glad you did. If you're dying for compliments, Facebook's got you covered! Why? Because both your friends and enemies are there, monitoring your progress. Perhaps they'll soon add a feature that will enable us add enemies, not just friends, that way you can separate your friends from enemies. Just kidding! But seriously, Facebook has changed the game in the social hemisphere. It has helped a lot of people overcome depression and driven some into it. Bitter-sweet uhn?

Instagram

If you think Facebook is intimidating, then you need to check out Instagram. Someone recently asked why everyone is always happy on Instagram. I checked and realized it's true. Not one drab picture. Almost every picture is a product of photo shoots – that's another angle; social media has opened a large market for photography. Gone are the days of Bola Photo Studios, now we have Elf Impressions. Photography is now a booming profession, all thanks to the 'pepper-dem-gangs' on social media. Instagram is a picture app that allows you share your pictures and videos on the go. This photo sharing social networking app enables you to capture the best moments of your life, with your phone's camera or any other camera, and convert them into works of art. And with the multiple filters, no one is ugly, trust me. It is the home of make-belief and many people have ridden on it to make their desired impressions on their desired audience. Businessmen and women have also hijacked the platform to sell their products and services. This has opened up a whole new world of branding. What's more, a lot of people now have careers just by teaching people how to sell on Instagram! Many 'coaches' are now springing up – health, fitness, fashion, business, social media, name it - and Instagram is their estate; they live there. It's a world of opportunities that keeps opening up.

WhatsApp

WhatsApp has been able to capture the attention of millions of people across the world by giving them the ability to communicate and share instantly with individuals and groups. Not just that, you can also do voice calls and video calls on WhatsApp. Who would have thought?! Just some years back, video calls were only seen in sci-fi movies. Now, it's a reality. The most important feature is perhaps the ability to chat infinitely. Unlike text messaging, where you are charged per text, WhatsApp offers you unlimited chatting. People have been known to be glued to their phones for hours, chatting away, even sleeping off while chatting. You're guilty too right? Ain't we all? And those broadcasts? Argggh!

Twitter

Twitter enables you to post short text messages (called tweets), containing a limited number of characters (up to 140), to convey your message to the world. Twitter is for more serious discussions, especially politics, and most politicians and even governments have a strong presence on Twitter. It's also a news hub, where you get news on the go. People also seize the opportunity of the traffic to advertise their goods and services. Nowadays, people don't even buy newspapers anymore because before the newspapers get the news, it's already on Twitter. News reporters now live on Twitter so as to get news on the go. This has greatly reduced news prints because the demand has dropped. And the way it's going, the 'paper' behind 'newspaper' will soon be dropped, because it will be strictly digital. Ever thought what would happen to newspaper vendors? That's another thought on the future of work.

Skype

Skype allows you to connect with people through voice calls, video calls (using a webcam) and text messaging. You can conduct group conference calls and hold meetings on Skype. Skype-to-Skype calls are free, all you need is internet. The best part is that it can be used to communicate with anyone, anywhere in the world as long as they have internet. Couples who leave apart can use this app to talk to each other daily at an almost zero cost. Gone are the days when couples will go and queue at NITEL (Nigeria Telecommunications Limited) offices to speak with their spouses. Now, you're able to see and hear each other instead of just hearing each other, as applicable in phone calls. If you know, you know (winks).

LinkedIn

LinkedIn is easily the most popular professional social networking app. It is available in over 20 languages. It is used across the globe by all types of professionals and serves as an ideal platform to connect with different businesses, locate and hire ideal candidates, build connections for freelance work, find potential partners, or simply to keep your job prospects open. So, before you complain to your child about being broke, have you tried increasing your visibility on LinkedIn?

Before we wind up here, would you like to know the most popular sites your children visit? I bet! The thing is, even if we don't know the intricacies of these apps and sites, we need to know the basics - what they are, why they're popular, and what problems can crop up when they're not used responsibly. Shall we? Cool!

Facebook:

The pictorial appeal of Facebook makes it endearing to our children. They are able to share their own pictures and stories as well as see others' own. It's a good way to spend their leisure. We need to watch out, as they also use it to binge, aspire and escape reality. It also exposes them to strangers you would want them protected from.

Group Me:

This is an app that doesn't charge fees or have limits for direct and group messages. Users can also send photos, videos, and calendar links. Not bad right? Don't relax just yet. Here is one thing you should know: the embedded GIFs and emojis have some adult themes, such as drinking and sex. Well, now you know!

Kik Messenger:

This app lets kids text for free. It's fast and has no message limits, character limits, or fees if you only use the basic features. Sounds innocent? Wait for it! Kik allows communication with strangers who share their Kik usernames to find people to chat with. The app allegedly has been used in high-profile crimes, and child-pornography. So, the next time you see this app on your child's phone or tablet, you know what to expect.

WhatsApp:

WhatsApp lets users send text messages, audio messages, videos, and photos to one or many people with no message limits or fees. Now, WhatsApp shouldn't be a problem, should it? No, but it could. Do you know it's for users above 16 years old? I didn't know either, until recently. Also, WhatsApp can be pushy. After you sign up, it automatically connects you to all the people in your address book who also are using WhatsApp and so there is the temptation to want to engage in unnecessary chats with strangers or semi-strangers. Now, you know what to do when your eight-year-old wants to chat on WhatsApp.

Instagram

Instagram lets users snap, edit, and share photos and short videos, either publicly or within a private network of followers. It unites the most popular features of social media sites: sharing, seeing, and commenting on photos. It also lets you apply fun filters and effects to your photos, making them look high-quality and artistic. This app is not suitable for children below age 16. Well, now you know it is inappropriate for your ten-year-old to open an Instagram account. You're welcome!

Tik Tok - Real Short Videos

This is a performance- and video-sharing social network that mostly features teens lip-synching to famous songs but also includes some original songwriting and singing. Users can build up a following among friends or share posts publicly. For teens who want a public profile to get exposure and approval, this is very appealing. It's not as harmless as it sounds, however. The songs and videos contain lots of swearing and sexual content. Even with teenagers, one needs to be on the lookout.

<u>**Tumblr:**</u>

This is like a cross between a blog and Twitter. It's a streaming scrapbook of text, photos, and/or video and audio clips. Users create and follow short blogs, or "tumblogs," that can be seen by anyone online (if they're made public). Many teens have tumblogs for personal use: sharing photos, videos, musings, and things they find funny with their friends. You should be on the lookout if your child visits this site. Why? Because despite it being hip and creative, pornographic images, videos and depictions of violence, self-harm, drug use, and offensive language are easily searchable. You see why you have to be digitally observant?

Live.me – Live Video Streaming

This app allows kids to watch others and broadcast themselves live, earn currency from fans, and interact live with users without any control over who views their streams. Sounds like fun, doesn't it? Not really. Kids can easily see inappropriate content like broadcasters cursing and using racial slurs, scantily clad broadcasters, young teens answering sexually charged questions, and more. Yeah, that bad!

Source: commonsensemedia.org

We can go on and on. However, the crux of the matter is that it's our duty as parents to be familiar with what our children are exposed to, online. Ignorance is never an excuse.

CHAPTER THREE

LET'S HAVE A CLEARER VIEW!

Last chapter was quite an eye opener, wasn't it? If you had a choice, you would throw away everything digital and just go back to our analogue world where things at least made some sense, not so? Don't be in a rush! There's more. Let's take a closer look at some of the many dangers the digital age poses for us and our children.

UNICEF broke down types of ICT dangers into three categories, called the three Cs: Content, Contact and Conduct. Content refers to the exposure to online material. Contact has to do with the child participating in adult-initiated activity. Conduct refers to the child being a victim or actor.

Now let's look at the different ways these are manifested, shall we?

Child Sexual Abuse and Exploitation

Moni (not real name) called her seven-year-old son who was sitting across her in the living room. David (not real name) did not answer. She called again and it was apparent he was so engrossed in the game he was playing on his tablet. She had just given him permission to download new games the day before. Moni moved closer to see what was so engrossing and got the shock of her life. The game was x-rated. It was about sexual conquests. She was speechless because she had no idea such games even existed. She thought all games were innocent; she had grown up with Nintendo games and had assumed every game fell into the same pattern. Well, she assumed wrongly! This is 2019 and games come in varied dimensions, many times highly sexual. She felt so guilty for exposing her son that way.

Moni is not alone on this table. A lot of us are actually not aware of the heavy sexual content inherent in the digital diet we feed our children. But as it has been said, ignorance is not an excuse. It is our duty to monitor our children's online activities. The world is no longer the secluded one we grew up in. Our children are exposed to many ills and we owe it to them to keep them safe. If we don't do it, who will? Another class is the nonchalant parents. They are aware of these dangers but they ignore them, thinking their children are sacred and well brought up, and therefore immune. I laugh in Greek.

Now, let's break down sexual abuse and molestation into the three Cs so that we can understand the full implications.

Content

This refers to unwanted and harmful exposure to pornographic content. Let's face it; sexual content has never been so accessible for both young and old. When we hear the cliché, "the world is a global village", let's be sure we know what it really means. One of its implications is that it is now as easy as ever for anyone, anywhere to be exposed to sexual content. In those days, we smuggled pornographic cartoons into our bags and God help us if our parents found them during routine bag checks. And we were well into our teens before we even knew those things existed. Wait a minute, do we even check our children's bags now? Just asking! Now, all our children need is a phone, tablet or laptop and they can access the core of pornography.

Contact

Do you know that while you're here grooming your child to be well-rounded and responsible, some people are scattered across the globe, scheming on how to reach your child and make him or her a participant in their devilish desires? Trust me, these guys ain't loyal! It is now easier for them to share images of their abuse and encourage each other to commit further sexual crimes. Let's not forget that pornography can be very addictive. What they really need is for your child to have contact with these sexual materials and viola, he or she becomes a victim. What's more, offenders can remain anonymous, cover their digital footprints, create fake identities, hunt many preys at once and monitor them.

Conduct

Once a child has had exposure to content and has been contacted, it is easy to become a regular consumer or actor. Take for example; if a girl is exposed to a dating site (content), she gets contacted by the owners and prospective dates (contact), next she becomes an active participant, always checking the site for prospective dates. That's conduct.

In David's case in the example at the beginning of this chapter, we can also see the three Cs play out. He was first exposed to the game, which is content. Then he participated in an adult initiated game, which was contact. Finally, he consistently consumed the sexual material, which is conduct.

Online sexual abuse and molestation as a result of online exposure is a very big issue. While some contents are meant for adults and children stumble on them, some sexual materials are deliberately designed to target children. We have a lot of perverts in the world now and the internet has made them one click away from our innocent children.

In the past, cases of child molesters were far and in between but it is a daily occurrence now. This is made worse by the internet. The internet promotes a high level of anonymity that helps fester sexual abuse of children. Abusers can now hide behind their screens and hunt their victims. This anonymity could also be a way of escape for our children. We all know how exciting it is to have a secret life. Many children see phones and other digital devices as a means of escaping reality. And to them, it is even more fun to have a stranger on the other side, someone unknown to their parents and other family members. This is worsened if a child is having problems at home. This type of child is easy target. The molester aims at buying the child's trust and making himself or herself look like a savior or guardian Angel. That is why it is very important to be very observant when it comes to our children.

A while ago, the story was told of a girl who started chatting with a stranger online. The man had everything a girl wants as could be deduced from the pictures he posted. The man promised to buy the girl a classy phone so that she could have better access to him instead of using her mother's phone to chat with him. Eventually, the guy bought the phone and told the girl to come and collect it at a hotel near her house. The girl went and your guess is as good as mine. There was no phone and the girl was brutally abused sexually, not by one guy, but three. All these went on without the parents' knowledge until things had gone really bad. This shows just how much damage a simple phone can cause if utmost care is not taken.

There was another story of a boy who was defiled by their maid. The mum was a busy executive who left him in the care of the maid. The maid would play all sorts of pornographic material and show them to the boy. Later, she started practicing them with him. The boy was only seven! See, things are happening and we could go on and on about digitally-induced sexual abuse. One thing has not changed though: It is our responsibility to protect our children from danger.

It's More Than Sex!

Any time we hear about dangers of the digital age, we often narrow it to sexual. It's more than sex, dear parent. There's a whole lot of danger out there beyond sexual abuse and molestation. Here are a few others!

Aggression and Violence

Eunice had always complained about her six-year-old being aggressive. The boy was always fighting with his peers and even adults. It was so bad that he would be boxing the air if there was nobody to box. His mother got really worried. She was afraid her lovely son was turning into a bully, or worse, a criminal. His parents were easy going and there were no traces of domestic abuse between them, so they wondered what the matter was. One day, Funke, Eunice's friend, came visiting and met the couple in the living room, watching a movie. James, their son, was also there. They started a discussion and soon, they were all reeling with laughter. It was Funke who noticed just how engrossed James was at the movie. She followed his gaze and it was an intense fight scene. It suddenly dawned on

Funke that that was the cause of the boy's aggression. Her parents were still busy laughing when she cut them short and told them to observe the boy. They still didn't get her point until she spelt it out for them. They had no idea action films were inappropriate for the boy. They felt as long as a movie didn't contain sexual scenes or innuendoes, he was free to watch it.

Are you like James' parents? Do you let your child watch movies and programs above his or her age grade? Do you justify it by saying it does not contain sexual content? Then I have news for you: You are playing with fire! Oh yes! You are exposing your child to self-abuse and self-harm, suicidal tendencies, discrimination and extremism. Children who are exposed to such violent and aggressive content have the tendency to give hate speech, discriminate, be involved in cyber-bullying and be radicalized (become terrorists). So, do you now agree with me that it's more than sex? That's not all, there's more where that came from.

Commercial Exploitation

Anne found out that the call credit on the phone her ten-year-old son used was quickly exhausted and he kept on asking her to recharge it. She always asked him what happened to the last recharge and he always said he used it to call his uncle. Anne raised her concerns with her colleague at work and he suggested she checked his browsing history, that it could be that he was using the airtime to browse. Anne didn't know one could browse without subscribing to a data plan. She only shared her WIFI with the phone when he wanted to download games and to her, that was the only source of data. She nevertheless made a mental note to check her son's browsing history when she got home. At home, she took the phone to check its browsing history and saw that the boy had only been visiting game sites and he did so only on days she shared her WIFI. So, the disappearing call credit still remained a mystery. She was about dropping the phone when something told her to check the call log and verify his calls to his uncle. She did and found that he rarely called his uncle with the phone. The times he had spoken with his uncle, it was his uncle who called, not him. Still puzzled, Anne decided to check the messages before subjecting the boy to questioning and in there, her answer was waiting. She saw messages upon messages from a gambling company. Her boy had been gambling and paying with call credit. She felt her leg give way under her.

Does Anne's story sound familiar? We can testify to how we get bombarded with messages from various lottery companies. Even our service providers are engaged in one lottery or the other, asking us to send a text to a number to win a large amount of money and that the text costs xxx amount. So, exposing a child to this without proper cautionary measures is opening him or her to commercial exploitation as well as the addiction that comes with betting or playing lottery.

Health Hazards

Although many of the claims regarding the health hazards related to the use of digital devices are not conclusive, it will be good to be cautious with the use of these devices, especially the way our children use them.

Using the mobile phone for hours may lead to mild or severe headaches. This I can testify to. Exposure to the rays of the phone for an extended period can cause strain on the eyes. Holding the phone or tablet for long can also cause wrist pains. It is therefore advisable to monitor the time our children spend holding the phone and being exposed to the light from the phone. Playing games, watching movies or chatting on the phone also requires sitting in one position for a long period of time. This may cause mild to severe joint pains. Allowing our children play games, chat or watch movies on the phone for hours is a no-no.

It is commonplace to see children, especially teenagers, use earphones. Some listen to music all day long, with the earpiece glued to their ears. We parents also do it. This should be stopped, please. It has been proven that extended use of the earpiece affects the ear drums and reduces our hearing abilities. Don't also forget that when your child uses earpiece, it becomes more difficult to monitor the music they are listening to. And trust me; with the trash out there being paraded as music, you do want to know the music they are feeding on. Majority of the trendy songs glorify sex, drugs and ill-gotten money.

What about mental health? We do not pay much attention to mental health in Africa. And this is so sad, given the rising rate of suicide among our youths. Before a child decides to take his or her own life, there has been a series of underlying issues left untreated. The phone aids and abets escapism. Many children use the phone to escape facing reality. Some suicide victims' social media handles have been scrutinized and traces of hopelessness have been seen in their posts but nobody took notice. The reason anyone would post suicidal messages on social media is usually because they have no trusted physical person to talk to in real life. We need to watch out and curb excessive attachment to digital devices in our children to avoid stories that touch. Escapism is a few steps from mental illness.

This caution is for everybody, really. The digital age has alienated families. Gone are the days of moonlight tales and family story time, now everyone is glued to one device or the other. One of the benefits of the analogue age is the bond families had, both at the nuclear and extended level. We went on holidays at cousin's places and family friends' houses; we had physical social lives. These occasions were also opportunities for parents and relatives to pass morals and societal values to children. Now, this is fast disappearing, if not fully disappeared. When was the last time you considered letting your child spend their holidays at a relative's or friend's place? Oh-oh! Most parents are wary of doing that because the world is now 'all man for himself'. If you monitor your child's media diet, do you know what the other child or children have been exposed to? Family and communal bond is fast disappearing, and guess who is mostly at the receiving end? Our children!

Before we leave this axis, here are other ills of the digital era:

- **Inability to relate with real people:** Because our children are so addicted to life online, they find it difficult to relate with real people. That's why we have many children lacking social skills because they spend most of their time with virtual people and characters. That is their reality and the real world is like a distraction to them.

- Loss of focus on education: Excessive use of digital devices will definitely have adverse effects on our children's education. You would see kids who know all the lyrics of the latest hip hop music but don't know their additions. Their minds are simply not into books. Why should it be? When there are so many fun things online. Some don't even want to go to school anymore. Why should they, when they can easily make money online. Isn't money the reason people go to school? We need to watch out.

- Impatience: Our children are very impatient and don't want to follow due process. Why, you ask? Because the internet is full of all sorts of short cuts and DIYs and these children feel everything in life has to be microwaved. They don't want to wait for anything, they want instant gratification. It's our duty to set them straight.

- Illusions about life: Kids nowadays think life is as glossy and flawless as what they see on TV and the internet. They see people looking accomplished with seemingly little or no efforts. They see the flashy cars, travels and trendy clothes of successful people. They don't see what happens behind the scenes and they're deluded. Due to this, they tend to desire things that are beyond their parent's income or reach. This puts a lot of pressure on parents and even the children themselves.

- Increase in bad usage of language: The digital world is a fast moving world and everybody is in a hurry. Everything is shortened or abbreviated now and almost everyone has caught the bug. The other day, a mother lamented that her son's teacher wrote a comment in her son's exercise book. She wrote: "Well done! U did a grt job!" Like seriously? The mother almost fainted. This was a teacher, for crying out loud. If a teacher could write like that in school, then what is the fate of the pupils? Almost everywhere you turn now on social media, you'll see 'You' being written as 'U', 'I'm' being written as 'Am', 'Come' being written as 'Com', 'Thanks' being written as 'Tnks'. I have a headache already. Don't you?

CHAPTER FOUR

ARE YOU STEPPING UP YOUR GAME?

Mum, You Need to Upgrade Your Phone

"Mum, when are you changing your phone?" asked Fausat, my seven-year-old daughter. I put the plate I was holding into the dish drainer and turned to look at her. "Why would I want to change my phone?" I asked quizzically, a puzzled frown gathering on my face. "Are you asking me, Mum?" she threw. "Your phone is outdated. It's too slow when browsing, it has little memory, it's not classy or trendy and it doesn't have many filters for photos," she finished. I gave her a long wry look I had inherited from my mother and shook my head accordingly, the same way my mum would do. What is this world turning into? I had no idea what a phone was when I was her age. I grew up in the village and the first time I saw an analogue telephone was in the university, in my HOD's office. The first phone I'd ever owned was a Nokia 3310 which I had to save for months to purchase. I had to thereafter wait for two more months to save up for the SIM card, which cost an arm and a leg. My dear daughter has never seen a Nokia 3310 phone before, which was the rave when all you needed a phone for was to call and send text messages. I doubt she knows what an analogue phone looks like. I definitely don't blame her when she calls my android old fashioned. She was born into the smartphone era. I can only shake my head.

-Tawa

No Jokes Dad, I Want to Be a Photographer

"Dad, I want to be a photographer," said Wole, my eleven-year-old boy. I laughed out loud. Wole, like me, had a huge sense of humor. He could make just about anyone laugh. As I drove out of our premises, I looked at the rearview mirror and saw that he was not laughing along as he would normally do when cracking jokes. Wait, was he serious? "Wole, that was a nice joke there, photographer indeed!" I shot. I needed to be sure this was a joke. "Dad, I'm not joking. I really want to be a photographer. I love taking pictures and I love good pictures when I see them," my son said in a way that knocked off all remnants of doubts in my mind. "Yeah, photography is not bad, but it's more like a hobby, okay? You should be thinking of careers in serious fields. Have you thought of engineering, architecture and medicine? Now, those are serious fields of study," I attempted to guide him. Who wouldn't want their child to become an architect, doctor or engineer? But photography? Excuse me! "Dad, photography is a great profession. There are many successful photographers," he squeaked. Oh my God! Where have I failed? Of all respectable professions in the world, it is photography that appeals to my brilliant son? It's like telling my parents when I was growing up that I wanted to be a musician. Now, that was more like an abomination. Where on earth did I get it wrong?

-Fred

Am I expected to use my hands?

My mother must be turning in her grave. My ten-year-old daughter can't wash her panties herself! She's becoming an adolescent and I'm teaching her personal hygiene and how she needs to wash her panties daily, instead of waiting till weekend when we use the washing machine. Can you believe she's insisting on running the washing machine to wash one panty? Unbelievable! I was shocked to my marrows. I wanted to give her a good spank before it dawned on me that she's never had to use her hands to wash clothes before. She was born into the washing machine age and there has never been a need to wash clothes with our hands. I wash my panties in our (my husband and I) bathroom and so she never even saw me wash with my hands. My mother must really be turning in her grave; she wouldn't believe a day would come that a ten-year-old descendant of hers would be unable to wash her own panties.

-Joan

The world has moved! Deal with it or get dealt with! One thing I've realized is that the world won't wait for you; you have to catch up with it. If you don't step up your game, you get knocked off the ring. A good place to start is for us as parents to have a major paradigm shift. We view the world from where we're coming from; our children view the world from what they're born into. We witnessed the evolution of smartphones and exotic tablets from analogue box phones; they opened their eyes as babies and saw smartphones and sleek tablets. We didn't see a computer until we were adults; they played with mini computers as babies. We woke up on Saturday mornings to piles of clothes and endless chores; they woke up to their favorite cartoons and games. We woke up on Saturdays to soak beans to be peeled and grounded on stone; they woke up to instant powdered beans to be mixed with water and fried. We trekked long distance to and fro school; they have chauffeur-driven, air conditioned cars, or public cabs and bikes to take them to and fro school. We were given all sorts of horrible punishments when we erred; they are not even allowed to be spanked. They lack a balance of the digital and non-digital experiences of life, which we have.

So, you see, they can't think like us. Their experience of the world is different. Their orientation and mentality regarding life is a whole world apart from ours. To make any progress with them, we need to view the world from their perspective. This will give us a balanced outlook. We cannot solve a new problem with an old solution, can we? That, however, is what a lot of parents do. We tend to solve our own parenting problems with the same approach our parents used for us. Little wonder we're not making much progress.

But how can we? It seems like it's only parents who have refused to step up their game in this digital age. Check out teaching, for example. Why are teachers not still referring pupils to encyclopedias and atlases? Why have they stepped up to digital-based teaching? Educators are daily responding to the needs of the digital generation rather than trying to fit a new generation into old models of education that they were taught with. A study by Jukes et al. (2010) reveals that more than 60 percent of students today are visual kinesthetic learners. This means they prefer learning that is relevant, active, instantly useful, and fun. They prefer to be engaged and discover course content through exploration, interaction, and collaboration. This is much different from our own model of learning which was mainly lecturing and cramming.

What about advertising? The content and channel of advertising has greatly changed from what we were used to. Adverts are now made around what people in this age can relate with. No advert will show a woman receiving a call from an analogue phone except it's a throwback. What about the channels? Now, we have adverts on Youtube videos, on our apps and even as text messages. Why don't advertisers limit their adverts to TV and Radio alone like they did when we were growing up? Because the world has moved and they have to catch up or be left behind! As a matter of fact, content and advertisement is now higher on new media than it is on traditional media.

Today, 'Mama Bisi' at the fabric market has an online presence. She posts pictures of her fabrics regularly on Instagram, Facebook and on her WhatsApp status. She doesn't just sit down in her shop; she realizes that her customers are now too busy to go to the market, but they are on social media. So, she does the smart thing and moves her beautiful fabrics to where they are. But she doesn't stop there; she gives them an option of delivery. That way, her customers don't have to move a muscle. At the clicks of their phones, they place their orders and have them delivered at their doorsteps. The bitter truth is that Mama Bisi is smarter than many parents. She refused to be stuck in the past. She realizes that the world has evolved and she also needs to evolve to survive. Many of us (parents) are still stuck in the past. We still use the old school model we were raised with, to raise our children and we complain of lack of results or contrary results.

Even churches are not left out of the evolution. Many churches don't wait for you to come to church now. They understand that the dynamics of society have changed and not everyone is free on Sundays anymore. So what do they do? They stream their services! Thus, you can attend church at work or on your bed, right from the comfort of your home. They have removed the walls in their churches; they now have websites. This also means their printing needs have reduced. Their content is now mostly digital. Not only that, their mode of advertising has evolved. They now invite people for programs through adverts on social media instead of strictly on radio and television as we were used to, while growing up. What do you think will happen to an urban church which still focuses solely on tracts and paper flyers as its evangelism and advertisement channels? It will not grow!

Let's bring it down home and look at the work you do. Is your mode of operation what it used to be ten years ago? Is your industry what it used to be, just ten years ago? Are your working tools what they used to be ten years ago? Are your customers limited to who they used to be ten years ago? Is your neighborhood what it used to be ten years ago? Is your spouse who he/she used to be ten years ago? I caught you there! Many couples never knew emotional affairs could occur in the dimensions they're now occurring, with the advance in technology. Many never knew their spouses could become great addicts of pornography, no thanks to the digital era. What about you? Are you the person you were, just ten years ago? Do you have the same tastes, preferences and friends you had ten years back? Ten years ago, I couldn't order goods or services from a random person on the internet, now I do! Ten years ago, I didn't make money from the internet, now I do! Ten years ago, I didn't hold classes and meetings virtually, now I do! So, if we can change the way we operate in other areas of our lives in just ten years, how come we're still trying to raise our children with the same methods our parents used thirty years ago? Think about it and remember this as you do: If you don't step up, you'll be stepped on.

CHAPTER FIVE

DON'T UNDERESTIMATE THE POWER OF EFFECTIVE COMMUNICATION

If after reading the last chapter, you're not ready to step up your game, I don't know if you'll ever be ready. The truth is we really don't have a choice if our intention is to raise well-rounded kids. Ready to step up your game? Great, let's do this!

When God stretches His hands...

"Mum, is it true that babies come from heaven?" Four-year-old Laraba asked her mum. "Yes, they do, my darling," her mum said with a sweet smile. "When you become a young woman and are ready to have a baby, God will stretch his hands from heaven and give you a beautiful baby," her mum added. "Did God stretch His hands to give me to you, Mum?" Laraba asked innocently. "Oh, yes my sweetheart. He sure did," said mum sweetly.

Does this sound familiar? I bet it does!

Jude, the Puncher

Jude and his dad were watching wrestling on TV. Jude is nine years old. "Daddy, that white man is so weak; he can't punch well at all. If it was me, I will punch his nose until it bleeds," Jude said with great excitement. "That's my boy! My no-nonsense boy," Jude's dad shouted as he rubbed his son's back, grinning as he focused his attention back on the game.

Is this also familiar? Are you Jude's dad or do you know a dad like Jude's?

No need to bother your pretty head, darling…

"Mummy, what is menstruation?" Six-year-old Lillian asked her mum as she hopped into the kitchen. Lillian's mum dropped the knife and onions she was holding on the kitchen cabinet and turned to face her daughter. "It's not for little children my darling," she said, squatting to look her eye to eye. "When you grow up, you will know all about it. So, don't bother your pretty head about adult things. Now, go get yourself some chocolates in the fridge," she finished.

Can you relate with this last example also? I can!

Now, what is wrong in the examples above? The first parent passed wrong information to her child. It's a classic case of misinformation. One of the dangers in this is that when the child learns the truth elsewhere, she will not trust her mother to tell her the truth again. She will gravitate towards her source of genuine information. For example, if she stumbles on a video or picture online which explains reproduction explicitly, she will always go online to get authentic information. Now imagine if she gets the info from an 'uncle' or the gateman? Oh, your guess is as good as mine!

In the second example, the parent communicated but was misleading. The father spoke with the son but encouraged him in the wrong path. He probably thought he was too young to carry out his 'punching desires' or he didn't see anything wrong in his son being violent. Either way, Jude now has daddy's permission to give James a bloody nose the next time he attempts to take the ball from him on the field.

The last example is a classic case of dismissal. Instead of telling the child the truth about the subject in the most appropriate way, the mother dismissed it and changed the conversation swiftly. This is a typical analogue way of handling issues. Our parents did it a lot. Instead of giving us information, they dismissed us as being too young, naïve or wayward. The main problem with this approach is that it overlooks the fact that children will always satisfy their curiosities, especially WiFi kids. So, if you dismiss them, they will keep on making enquiries until they find the answer. And when they do, you may not be able to control how they utilize the information. Why? Because nowadays, most information sources also give you options of utilizing those info.

Let's settle this once and for all: If you miss it with your children in communication, you have missed it indeed! One major way to raise well-rounded kids in this digital age is to be able to communicate with them and they, with us, effectively. We need to not only be able to communicate with them; we need to communicate with them effectively. A lot of crisis we have with our children could have been prevented by building a foundation of proper communication. Now, while each child and family is different, there are basic communication skills we all must adopt to communicate effectively with our children. Let's have a look!

Not so fast! Let's quickly agree on what effective communication involves, so we're sure we're on the same page. Is that okay? Fantastic! Good communication with children is about:

- encouraging your children to tell you about their thoughts and feelings;
- the ability to really listen and respond in appropriate ways to not just nice gist or pleasant news, but also rage,

tantrums, humiliation or embarrassment, grief, alarm, etc.;

- having knowledge and understanding of what children of different ages have the ability to understand;
- having knowledge of the attention span of children of different ages and temperaments;
- monitoring their body language and taking note of their tone and words so as to get a better understanding of what they are saying.

Encouraging our children to talk to us about their thoughts and feelings is probably the most important factor in effective communication. The reason is simple, isn't it? If they don't talk to us, they will talk to someone else! And that someone else may not have our children's interests at heart, and even if they do, they can't be as concerned about our children like us. Hence, you're the best person for your child to open up to. A lot of parenting problems stem up from the child not being able to talk to his or her parents. This definitely is one of the characteristics of analogue parenting. Most of us were scared of discussing certain issues with our parents. Some of us couldn't even sit down and have any kind of discussion with our parents. The major reason for this is the popular saying then that, "children are to be seen and not heard." And so, many children swallowed all their thoughts and feelings until they met someone who was willing to listen and most times, it led to dangerous consequences. If it led to dangerous consequences then, what do you think it leads to now, when children can get all the attention they want online? Some of us are even so comfortable leaving our children to 'get busy' online so we can also have time to 'get busy' online. We use phones and other gadgets to engage our children because we don't want to be disturbed. My two cents: Be disturbed now so you don't have to be greatly disturbed in future.

We need to encourage our children to open up to us. How do we do this?

- ***Be available***: The first thing we need to do is to be available! This is probably the most important step we need to take in order to communicate effectively with our special ones. How can you communicate in absentia? Trust me, some of us do! We're often busy chasing money in such a way that we don't have time for our children. And the little time that remains after chasing money is spent online. Raise your hands if you're guilty of this (smiles). Let's also note that being available differs: you can be physically available and not be mentally and emotionally available! You can even be financially available and be absent physically, emotionally and mentally. See what I'm saying about effective communication being a little complex in this era? A lot of parents are physically available but not mentally and emotionally available; therefore, their children can't approach them for a discussion.

- ***Be willing:*** Some parents are available but are not willing to talk to their children. Like Lillian's mum, they are quick to dismiss their children's quest to talk. We see that every day, don't we? We see a mother or father shutting their child up when he or she wants to talk or has an opinion. Even when we don't have the answers, we shouldn't shut them up, we should lovingly let them know we don't have the answers and we will find out. Don't shut your child up! One thing we should know is this: Children will talk anyway, but it may not be to you. They will talk to a friend, a foe, a stranger (online or offline) or to themselves. And the consequences are not usually pleasant. The beauty of this is that you have a choice to be the one your child talks to and this choice is your best option. Be willing!

- ***Be open to talk about anything:*** Life is a mix of the good, the bad and the ugly. Unfortunately, you can't choose your mix, and I say this within context. There will be things that are not favorable that you just have to deal with. So, sometimes your child may tell you things that are not palatable or things you'll rather not discuss. Don't shut them up or skip the matter and jump to another issue. Never sweep issues under the carpet with your children! Make sure you discuss everything they raise with you, especially serious and sensitive issues. When you scold them or shut them up when they bring serious issues or unpalatable issues up, they won't discuss them with you again, but you can be sure they will discuss them with someone else.

- **_Talk about your own experiences:_** When you open up to your children, they will be free to open up to you also. When you talk about your challenges when you were their age, they will be encouraged to talk to you about their present challenges. When you show them your vulnerability, they will be vulnerable with you too.

- **_Schedule time for talking_**: Isn't it funny that we schedule time for work, for the spa, for the hairdresser's, for the gym, for parties, even for time out with friends but we never schedule time to talk to our jewels. We don't think it's important, do we? Most of us need to prioritize the activities in our lives. The friend you're hanging out with won't take the place of your child if you raise a dysfunctional child. Your office or business won't compensate you if your child turns out badly. The people whose party you attend with so much vigor on a regular basis won't associate with you if your child becomes a disgrace. Your sexy body won't matter when your child is sexually molested. All the money you're chasing now won't make any difference at a certain level of damage. Make time for what is important now. Schedule time to have intimate talks with your children and bond with them!

- ***Talk regularly about general things:*** We all know how easy it is to open up to someone you talk to regularly, unlike one you rarely talk to? Good! Talk regularly about general things with your children, it will make it easier to talk about sensitive issues. When you talk about school, their friends, the family's welfare, country, etc., it will make it easier to transition into deeper talks like sexuality and feelings. The only time some of us have any talk with our children is when it comes to sensitive issues, e.g. when they didn't do well in school, when they bully a classmate, when they are found in sexually compromising situations, etc. If this is the case, your child will always be tensed any time you decide to talk to him or her, and that is not effective communication.

- ***Judge not:*** Don't judge them when they tell you unpleasant things. When you become dramatic or judgmental when your child tells you unfavorable things, you're shutting them up. Be calm even when you're boiling inside. When you flip your lid, you alarm your child and he or she won't be free to open up their innermost pains to you anymore. Chastise when you need to do so but do it with love. Don't discourage them from telling you about sensitive or unpleasant issues.

Communication is a very wide topic that can't be completely covered in the framework of this book. I'll advise you pick up a couple of communication books and master the art of communicating effectively with your children. However, here are some tips you will find useful if your aim is to communicate effectively with your children.

- Make eye contact while talking to your child. This builds trust and shows you're sincerely interested in what he or she is saying.

- Leave all you're doing and focus all attention on your child while he or she is talking to you. Some of us are fond of pressing our phones while having conversations with our children. What this tells them is that the phone or whatever you're doing on the phone is more important than them. Put yourself in their position and have someone use the phone while you're having a conversation you consider very important and see how you'll feel.

- Prompt your child to talk to you. Ask leading and open-ended questions that will make him or her talk more about their deepest thoughts and feelings.

- Don't jump in or cut them short or put words in their mouths. Don't be in a hurry to complete their sentences, let them find the right words to express their thoughts.

- Watch out for their body language and facial expressions. This will help you know if they're hiding stuff from you or lying. For example, a child who avoids eye contact with you while giving a report is probably hiding some details or lying.

- Don't be quick to provide solutions or fix their problems so you can terminate the conversation. Sometimes, all they want is your company and a listening ear.

- Make instructions and requests simple and clear. Let them match your child's age and ability.

- Model the right form of communication for your child. They do what they see us do, not what we tell them to do. If you interrupt people rudely in conversations, your child will do the same. If you avoid eye contact when talking to others, your child will pick the cue.

- Give your children a chance to respond when you talk to them, you're not a lecturer. Communication is two-sided: you talk and then you listen and vice versa.

- Seize opportunities to talk while doing other tasks together. If you have a very busy schedule, you can talk while taking your child to school, while bathing or while shopping.

- Reflect your child's feelings by repeating what they have just said. Let empathy show in your voice and expression as you do this.

I hope you've gained a thing or two from this chapter. Like any other skill, you get better at communicating with your child with practice. Thank me later. Or you can thank me now.

CHAPTER SIX
WHERE ARE THE BOUNDARIES?

"The most dangerous thing we can do for youngsters nowadays is to deny them access to the digital world. But the second most dangerous thing is to give them unlimited access."

- Donald Shifrin

When your house is 'da bomb' (pun intended)

"Men! You need to see the new hot video Lil Wayne just dropped," ten-year-old Uche said to Saheed as they stepped out of the class. "Wow! Has he dropped it already? I thought it was coming out next week," Saheed said, his eyes rolling with excitement. "No, o. You this boy, you're not current at all," Uche threw at his friend, shaking his head. "Yes, I know I'm not as current as you. You know my mum doesn't allow us watch the cool music channels," said Saheed. "Hmmm, that your mum! When will she 'wake up' like my mum? This new video dropped at 12 midnight and I downloaded it at 12:03," Wale boasted with a wide smile. "Wow! How did you do it? How did your parents allow you to stay up that late? And where did you get data to download it?" Saheed asked, his eyes enlarging like balloons. Uche burst into laughter. "Have you forgotten I don't live in your house? I told my dad I needed to download the new video and he let me use his WiFi. Simple!" Saheed's eyes were about to pop out of their sockets. "Men! Your house is da bomb!"

If you're Uche's parent, congratulations! You're about to have a crisis on your hands very soon. No, I'm not being negative, it's simple projections. If your ten-year-old has access to the internet at midnight when you're probably sleeping, you can be double sure he's checking out some other stuff. And trust me, they're not cartoons.

And if you're Saheed's parent, don't gloat just yet. Even if you create boundaries at home, don't forget your son still gets to see these videos on Uche's phone in school – as well as other stuff Uche gets to download. So, you see why all hands must be on deck to create healthy boundaries in this WiFi age?

That's what's in vogue!

"Mama Becky, please look at this style very well. That's the style my daughter wants to use for her birthday. Make sure you help me sew it well, please. Which fabric will be most suitable?" Julie's mum said with excitement to her tailor. "Ma, don't you think this style is too revealing for an eight-year-old girl? I mean, this exposes the chest, laps and back," said Mama Becky, her brows crouching, showing great concern. "Not at all, it is not revealing at all. That's what's in vogue now. This is the picture of her favorite social media influencer and my daughter has specifically said that's the style she wants for her birthday. And I promised to satisfy her on her birthday. You know it comes only once a year," said Julie's mum dismissively. "Yes, Ma," said Mama Becky, hiding her shock and disapproval.

To all the Mama Julies, I say well done. The food you're cooking will soon 'done'. It's only a matter of time. I only hope you will be able to eat it by the time it's ready.

If I stop now, I will never win…

"Dave, have you done the dishes?" Dave's mother asks as she looks up from her phone to check the time. It was 6pm. Nine-year-old Dave had been playing games on his phone since he came back from school. "Mum, please let me finish playing this level, if I stop now, I will never win," Dave told his mum, his eyes fixed on the game. "Okay o," said his mother as she continued chatting with her friend. One hour later, she looked up from her phone and Dave was still playing the game. "Dave!" she screamed. "You're still playing that game, it's seven o'clock." Dave, with his back still turned to his mother repeated, "Mum, please let me finish playing this level, if I stop now, I will never win." His mother just shook her head and proceeded to the kitchen to do the dishes.

I have no words for Dave's mother. Sincerely, I don't! All I have for her is sympathy.

I would yell too…

Mother: Doctor, I don't know what the matter is. My son keeps yelling and fretting.

Doc: Oh, really? When did it start?

Mother: It's been going on for weeks now.

Doc: Okay, how old is he?

Mother: He's a year old.

Doc: Okay. Does he have a particular time he yells?

Mother: Yes, Doctor. Each time there is power outage or we switch off the generator or I take him away from my laptop.

Doc: Okay. What activity is he always engaged in before there is power outage?

Mother: He's either watching TV or a Youtube video on my laptop.

Doc: Oh! How many hours does he spend watching TV or videos on your laptop?

Mother: Like 7-8 hours a day. It keeps him occupied while I do chores around the house.

Doc: I see. I would yell too if I were he.

Okay, maybe the doctor wouldn't have responded that way but I definitely would have. What are you thinking?! Having a baby spend his life in front of screens? That baby is having addiction issues. Don't let this shock you, it is commonplace now. Research has it that 38% of children under age two have used a mobile device for playing games, watching videos or other media-related purposes (mashable.com). Oh, oh!

Let's face it, one of the major keys to raising wholesome kids in this era is to create healthy digital boundaries. Now, what exactly are digital boundaries and why do we need to create them? Digital boundaries are limits we put to our children's exposure to digital media. The reason we need to do this has already been highlighted in earlier chapters. So, while exposure to digital media is good, we must ensure it is not too much so as to avoid stories that touch. And as technology keeps evolving, we have a duty as parents to keep rewriting the rules; it isn't business as usual, Dear Parent. So, how can we create boundaries as parents to WiFi kids?

- ***Have Family Values:*** This perhaps is the most important step in setting boundaries for your child. Your child must know that certain behaviors and attitudes are not allowed in your home. This will make it easier for you to control the content you allow and also make it easier for your child to understand why he or she cannot watch certain movies, play certain games, watch certain musicals or sing certain lyrics. Your family values will always be a guide even when you're not there.

- ***Regulate screen time:*** Have a maximum period your child can spend on the screen, whether TV, phone, laptop or tablet, per day. Create a DDD (Daily Digital Dose) for your children. Some of us allow our children to watch TV endlessly, sometimes late into the night, even on a school day! We've turned our devices into babysitters. Anytime we want to work or get 'busy' on our own devices, we engage them with a 'pacifier' and leave them with these devices for hours. This is wrong. Research has shown that children should spend more time having real conversations with people than playing games, chatting or watching movies.

- ***Prioritize:*** Let your children know some tasks and chores are more important and therefore come before screen time. Let them know they need to do certain tasks or activities before they are allowed to watch their favorite program on TV or play that game. Let them know there are certain hours they can't watch TV or play games because those hours are dedicated to more important things. This doesn't have to be limited to chores and duties but may include other activities that they find enjoyable, like crafts, reading, or indoor and outdoor activities.

- ***Get digital education:*** There are some boundaries that you need to set digitally. An example is having a password on your phone and even changing them regularly. These kids are very smart and may guess your password and access your phone in your absence. You also must be able to check the history on your devices. This way, you have an idea of what your child has been up to online. There are apps now that enable you monitor your child's digital footprints anywhere you are. Find out about them. You also need to be familiar with games and movies that are appropriate for your kid. You should know where to get these materials and not just leave your child to be sourcing the web for games and movies. Video games that reward aggression and promote violence and crime should be banned. You can't know all of these except you're digitally savvy yourself, can you?

- ***Provide alternatives:*** When you limit your child's screen time, what is he or she supposed to be doing during those periods? Good question! Find interesting and engaging activities to keep them occupied. Don't let your child miss screen time so much because there aren't fascinating activities off screen. If this is the case, he or she would begin to see the digital space as the ideal world. Also, download educational games and material that will limit the quest for indecent material.

- ***Physician, heal thyself:*** You can't draw boundaries for your child and fail to do same for yourself. A lot of us spend hours on end, chatting and just lazing away on social media, yet we expect our kids to respect the boundaries. Sorry buddy, but it doesn't work that way. Model the change you wish to see. I know sometimes we work or read on our phones. When that is the case, explain to your children and let them know what you're doing so they don't think you're just having fun for many hours on your phone while forbidding them to do the same.

- ***Create Tech-free Zones:*** Create rules not to have phones or devices while eating. Another way you can do this is also to not put televisions in the bedrooms. Having televisions in bedrooms, especially your children's, may encourage watching TV at inappropriate times. You can also make rules not to use devices in the rooms; everyone should use their devices in the living room where others can see what they're doing.

- ***Don't leave your WiFi on***: Some parents leave their WiFi permanently on and every member of the family can use the internet at anytime. Don't do this; have designated periods when you can monitor your child's online activities.

There are many other ways we can create boundaries in our homes in order to raise well-rounded kids. Find out what works for you. What matters is that you're making conscious efforts to ensure the WiFi age becomes an advantage and not a disadvantage for you and your child.

CHAPTER SEVEN

CREATING AND MAINTAINING EFFECTIVE SLEEP PATTERNS

Teacher: Welcome Mrs. Akpan. Hope you're fine.

Mrs. Akpan: Good morning Mrs. Ade. I'm fine. Thank you.

Teacher: Great! I told you to come see me so I can draw your attention to certain observations.

Mrs. Akpan: Okay. Hope Joe has not been up to any mischief?

Teacher: Not at all Madam. I notice he sleeps in class sometimes and hardly concentrates. This is affecting his grades.

Mrs. Akpan: Oh, really?

Teacher: When asked what time he sleeps, he said 12am!

Mrs. Akpan: No way! I send him off to bed at 9pm. Please call him for me.

Joe was summoned.

Mrs. Akpan: Joe, your teacher here said you told her you don't sleep until 12am. Don't I send you off to sleep at 9pm?

Joe: Yes mummy.

Mrs. Akpan: So, why did you say you don't sleep until 12 am?

Joe: (looking down at his feet) Because I play games on my tablet until late at night.

Mrs. Akpan: Chisos!

If there is any aspect of health and wellness that this WiFi era has affected, it is our sleep pattern. It has become a general cause for concern for everyone but it is of more concern for us as parents, regarding our children. We didn't have this problem, growing up. Why? Because back in the day, the national- and state-owned TV stations resumed at 4pm and closed at 10pm after the Network News. There were no video games; we made do with Nintendo games and board games which were well rationed because we needed time to do chores and homework. There definitely was no internet and you didn't have anything to browse, late into the night. We didn't have social media and there was no one to chat with late at night; the only people who had nocturnal chats with 'virtual' people in those days were witches! And yes, I'm of the opinion that African witches be given credit for virtual chats and meetings, they started it first; they just didn't have the technology or propensity to share it with the world. Just kidding!

But seriously, our lives were much simpler and quite regulated, unlike what obtains now; 24-hour TV – with inexhaustible channel options, internet that opens the world to you and opens you to the world, social media that allows you to catch up on gist and gossip, do business, develop many relationships, relate with strangers, etc. We can never get tired of comparing these two periods, can we? It's because the difference is clearer than 7UP and we need the constant comparative analysis to remind us of just how different life is now and how parenting methods and approaches must also differ.

No doubt, these new technologies have disrupted our sleep patterns. Many of us now sleep with our phone in hand. Research has shown that most adults pick up their phones at approximately five seconds after they wake up. Our phones have become a serious addiction that some of us need therapies for. And it is not without its side effects, one of which is the disruption of sleep patterns. This is more so for children who are at their developmental age and need all the sleep they can get. I remember us having siesta while growing up. How many homes observe siesta nowadays? How can they, when nobody is even at home in the afternoons? Parents are at work and children are still in school or in one after-school facility! When they get home at night, everybody either watches the TV or picks up a gadget and these occupy them late into the night. The next morning, they're up early to start the day and this becomes the cycle. This is more so in our metro cities. It's a rat race, really, with the resultant effect on the health, growth and performance of our children.

At MummyClinicc, we get a lot of cases from mothers who have issues getting their kids to sleep and when we dig deep down, we find out that TV and other gadgets are at the root of majority of these problems. And this sleep issue is no respecter of age; it affects children of ages 0-18. We found out in the course of relating with these mothers that a lot of parents don't know the importance of sleep and they also don't know that children need more sleep than adults, so they take it for granted until they begin to see the consequences. See, sleep is like food. When you don't eat, your body craves for it and when you deny it further, it starts to manifest with different adverse reactions. It's the same with sleep. When you deny your body the needed amount of sleep, it starts to tell on your health and productivity, which in turn affects the quality of life you live. We all know how grouchy and short fused we are when we don't get enough sleep, yet we take it for granted and deny our children the adequate amount of sleep needed. But eh, do we even know the amount of sleep our children need per age? Well, as a sleep consultant, it is my job to know and also ensure that you, as a parent, know.

According to the American Academy of Pediatrics, below are the recommended sleep hours for children, per age.

- Infants under 1 year: 12-16 hours
- Children 1-2 years old: 11-14 hours

- Children 3-5 years old: 10-13 hours
- Children 6-12 years old: 9-12 hours
- Teenagers 13-18 years old: 8-10 hours

Some of us are very good cheaters. You know yourself! But one thing we can't cheat is nature. It may look like we're getting away with many things we should take care of or pay attention to, as regards our lifestyles. However, one day, the consequences will catch up with us and it's not likely to be palatable. It may even be too late. Now, let's find out the consequences of lack of proper sleep for our children.

Irritability is one of the effects of lack of sleep. When your baby or child is touchy and bad-tempered, you need to check his or her sleep patterns. An irritable child is impatient and always on edge. This affects their work and play and their relationship with others. It affects you also.

A child with inadequate sleep is forgetful. Their brain is craving for sleep and wants to shut down so it cannot retain much information. This affects their performance in school, obviously. So, if your child's grades have been dropping, you may need to check his or her sleep patterns.

When you observe that your child is hyperactive, you may need to examine how well he or she sleeps. When a child doesn't get enough sleep, he or she is unsettled. This is more so if the brain has been active when it should be sleeping. Therefore, the brain has been reconfigured to be active, thereby making the child restless. Letting your child have unlimited access to gadget can cause this. We parents need to be on the lookout.

Limited attention span and lack of concentration are effects of lack of sleep. When a child is watching TV or playing games when he or she is supposed to be sleeping, it leads to short attention span. The child is unable to focus on anything for long and this affects his or her studies, health and life generally.

The impact of lack of sleep on our children cannot be overemphasized. According to the NHS in the UK, new brain scans reveal sleep deprivation damages children's brains. The study was carried out by researchers from a good number of institutions including the University of Colorado and University Hospital Zurich. Wow, right? You never knew it was this serious? Well, now you do!

Depression and many behavioral problems in children have also been linked to lack of proper sleep. We can go on and on about the disadvantages of sleep, however, let's do a flip and see the benefits of a good sleep pattern.

A good sleep spurts growth in children. We must have heard that children grow while they sleep and probably discarded it as a myth. Actually, this is true. Studies have shown that growth hormone is primarily secreted during deep sleep. Italian researchers, studying children with deficient levels of growth hormone, have found that they sleep less deeply than average children do (parents.com). Therefore, if you want proper growth for your child, be sure to let him or her have the required sleep per day.

Another merit of letting your child have adequate sleep is that sleep helps your child battle diseases. During sleep, children (and adults) produce proteins known as cytokines, which the body relies on to fight infection, illness, and stress.

When your child gets enough sleep, he or she is less likely to have injuries. "One study of Chinese children found those who were short sleepers (i.e., fewer than nine hours per night for school-age children) were far more likely to have injuries that demanded medical attention. And 91 percent of kids who had two or more injuries in a 12-month period got fewer than nine hours of sleep per night" (parents.com).

Also, a good sleep pattern improves your child's learning abilities, which in turn affects his or her school performance. When your child sleeps well, he or she is able to concentrate more on their studies and retain most of what is being taught.

So, before you scold that child and call him or her a dullard, you need to check their sleep habits.

What about the benefits for you as a parent? If you have a baby, you'll have lesser sleep disruption that occurs because your child can't sleep. Also, you'll have time to do other things when your child is asleep. You can read a book, do a course, or even spend more time with your partner. What's more, you have fewer things to worry about! You don't want to know how much money parents whose kids have sleep defects spend to get remedies. What about the stress and emotional impacts? Huge!

How then can we create an effective sleep pattern for our WiFi kids? No doubt, this is a big task we have as parents in the WiFi era. Our own parents didn't have this kind of challenge, but then, they also didn't have the benefits of the digital age we now enjoy. So you see, win some, lose some!

First you need to find out the required sleep hours for your child and set a bedtime with it, taking your lifestyle into consideration. If you have to leave home by 6am and your children have to be awake by 5am, you know you have to calculate the number of sleep hours required and count back for you to get the ideal bedtime. This means they probably have to sleep earlier than the children of someone who leaves home by 8am or who works from home. You also need to note that your children's sleep requirements are not the same as yours. A lot of my clients make that mistake. They send their children to sleep only when they are feeling sleepy and they wake them up at the same time. This is wrong. You require less sleep than your child and you shouldn't use your own sleep requirements as a yardstick.

Have bedtime routines. Little success is achieved in life without routines. Successful people are those who have made productive habits a routine. The same principle applies to creating efficient sleeping patterns. Create a series of activities that announce bedtime and your child will find it easier to sleep. As you carry out these activities daily, they give a signal to the body that it is time to shut down and you will find it easier to put your children to sleep.

Be consistent! Keep regular sleep and wake up times. Don't put your child to sleep at different times of the day. Don't do 8pm today and 10pm tomorrow. Don't wake them up at 5am today and 7am tomorrow. When you're inconsistent with these timings it makes it difficult to have a sleep pattern. If there are going to be discrepancies, ensure it is not more than 30 minutes, give or take.

Taking a warm bath before sleep can make it easier for your child to sleep. A warm bath soothes, refreshes and calms. It makes the body relax and ready to wind up. So, the next time your child is finding it difficult to sleep, you may want to try a warm bath.

Having a conducive room is critical to a good night's sleep. We all know how difficult it can be to sleep if the room is not comfortable; even if one is feeling sleepy, it will be difficult to really relax and sleep if the room is not in order. Ensure your child's room is well ventilated and the temperature balanced; not too airy or cold and not too warm. Check the lighting, some children like the lights on before they sleep, some don't. Find out what works for your child. Having a dim light has proven to be effective. What about the noise? If you're in Nigeria and generator noise is the norm, you may need to move your child to a room with less exposure to this noise, failure to do so may result in lack of sleep. Toys may be a distraction as your child may not want to sleep if there is the option of playing with a toy. Endeavor to remove all toys that can distract. On the other hand, your child may find a particular toy soothing and cuddly and may want to have it around; indulge such a child if the end result is a good night's sleep.

Reduce screen time and shut all screens at least two hours before bedtime. Children who spend too much time before screens have been found to have difficulties sleeping. Also, our bodies and brains need to relax before sleep time, therefore, watching TV, playing games or streaming online immediately before bedtime will only extend bedtime. The brain will not wind up immediately after screen time, it needs some time. So, make allowance for this time. Your child can read a storybook, listen to soothing music or chat with you during this period.

Don't feed your child too close to bedtime. A lot of modern parents do this a lot due to their work schedules. They get back from work late, cook, eat and send the children to sleep almost immediately because they're trying to save time. Research has shown that your child may find it difficult to sleep when this is the case. This may lead to indigestion and other related discomforts that will not allow your child have a good night's sleep.

In relation to the above, do not give your child too much food and too little food before sleeping. Always ensure your child eats before sleeping. An overfed child will find it difficult to sleep, likewise a hungry child. Creating a balance is key.

Avoid giving your child caffeine before sleep. In fact, don't give your child caffeine in the couple of hours before bedtime. Please be reminded that caffeine is in many soft drinks and 'juices' we give our children. Caffeine disrupts sleep.

Make out time to put your children to sleep. Find out what makes your child sleep faster and do it for him or her. For some children it is reading them a story, for others, it is singing them a lullaby. You will also find out that sleep time is a good time to bond with your little darlings. Some parents just send their children to their rooms and they go to theirs, assuming that the child will sleep immediately. We can see that in the case of Joe above. His mother assumed he slept at the time he went to his room but she never checked to be sure he did. While you may not need to sing a lullaby to older children, ensure you check to see they have actually slept.

Ban all devices from room. Joe's mother also made this mistake. She allowed her son to have a tablet with him in his room. We all know how difficult it is to let go of our phones when it is time to sleep, why do we assume it's going to be easy for our children? Ensure the room is stripped of all distracting devices that may keep your child awake at night.

Avoid allowing your children watch horror and violence movies. Make sure your child watches only age appropriate movies. Exposing them to horror and violence could deter them from sleeping well. Many children have nightmares and are unable to sleep again because of what they have seen during the day. Some have disturbing thoughts all through the night as they try to process what they've watched.

While children and families are different, following the above guides will generally help our children sleep better and harness the benefits of a good sleeping habit. And this is very necessary if we're raising well-rounded kids in this WiFi age.

CHAPTER EIGHT
LET'S TALK ABOUT SEX!

Mum: Joan, you're not a small girl again. It's high time we talked about sex.

Joan: Okay, Mum. What do you want to know about sex?

Mum faints!

Really, I can't say I blame Joan's mum. Imagine the shock of discovering your supposed innocent daughter, whom you want to start introducing to sex education, has a PhD in it and can even lecture you. Melodramatic as the above scenario may look, it is reality. Our WiFi kids know more stuff about sex than we may ever know. Gone are the days of "...and Adam knew his wife." Sexual issues are on another level nowadays and we must handle it with equal magnanimity. In our days, sex was described as "meeting", "sleeping with", "laying with" or "knowing". All of those terms are absolutely outdated now and for you to give your children proper sex education and supervision, you need to upgrade your analogue brain. Oh yeah! Okay, let's do a brief updating. You do know some social media abbreviations/slang, don't you? I'm guessing you know the following already:

UWC: You're welcome

LOL: Laughing out loud

ROTFL: Rolling on the floor

LMAO, now *LEEMAO*: Laughing my ass off

BRB: Be right back

TTYL: Talk to you later

SMH: Shaking my head

Now, let me blow your mind. What about these ones?

IWSN: I want sex now

PIR: Parent in room

99: Parent gone

1174: Party meeting place

420: Marijuana

POS: Parent over shoulder

LsMIRL: Let's meet in real life

TDTM: Talk dirty to me

LH6: Let's have sex

411: Info

53X: Sex

THOT: That Hoe Over There

KOTL: Kiss on the lips

PRON: Porn

8: Oral Sex

IPN: I'm posting nudes

WTTP: Want to trade pictures?

DOC: Drug of choice

GYPO: Get your pants off

KPC: Keeping parents clueless

(Courtesy: Kelly Wallace. CNN Correspondent)

Did I blow your mind or not? I bet I did! I particularly liked the last one: KPC: Keeping Parents Clueless. How apt! These are stuff your children don't want you to know. Unfortunately, some parents are keeping themselves clueless. Instead of seeking knowledge and looking for ways to match the tempo of the WiFi age, they're busy playing ostrich. See, gone are those days when what you don't know cannot kill you, these days, nothing kills faster. You need to know! Say to yourself five times: I refuse to be clueless! Three times is fine, really. Just kidding! But seriously, we cannot afford to be clueless parents in this WiFi age.

It's crystal clear now that we cannot approach sex education with our kids the way our parents did. Some of us did not even have any sex education from our parents, we learnt from outsiders in very unpleasant ways. Our children are exposed to sexual images and innuendoes right from the cartoons they watch. Forget it; these cartoons are not in the league of Tom and Jerry or Voltron. Seemingly harmless cartoons that we expose our toddlers to, have underlining subtle sexual engineering. What about the scourge of pornography? At the click of buttons now, kids have access to all sorts of pornography sites and we know just how addictive porn can be. Great precautions have to be taken, Dear Parent, because whether you face it or not, the digital age is a game changer!

How do we now navigate this terrain? How do we have conversations about sex with our kids in this digital era? At what stage do we start talking to them about sex? How much information do we reveal to them per time? How do we guide them from being exposed to sexual information beyond their age grade? How do we supervise and ensure they don't cross their bounds? Come with me!

Before you can have effectual sexual conversations with your child, you need to have a good communication relationship with him or her. If you need to read the chapter on communication again, kindly do so. It is easier to discuss a sensitive issue like sex with a child you already have good rapport with. There's no way a child you scold or dismiss or hardly have time for, will feel comfortable discussing sex with you. Thus, the first step is to create an atmosphere of smooth communication in your home.

Next, you need to know sex education is all encompassing. It isn't just about the act of sex, it is the totally of our sexuality. This involves topics like puberty, reproduction, sexual intercourse, sexually transmitted diseases, unwanted pregnancy, chastity and other personal, family and societal expectations.

There are two types of sexual education in this digital age. The first is the abstinence-only sexual education. This is when we teach our children the need to wait until marriage or until they become adults before they have sexual relations. This therefore does not cover information of birth control and the prevention of STDs. Instead of this, we let our children know the risks involved in premarital sex, both physically and psychologically and what they can do to abstain from it.

The second type of sexual education is the health and safety-oriented sex education. This is when you teach your child the basics of sex as well as birth control and when to and when not to give sexual consent. The justification given for this type of sexual education is so that children may be able to protect themselves in situations where they cannot discuss with their parents or any adult. For example, if a girl is raped and she is too traumatized to tell her parents, she would know what to do to prevent unwanted pregnancy and sexually transmitted diseases.

You may choose the type of sex education you want to give your child depending on the age of your child, your personal and family values, as well as the sexual orientation of the child in question. However, for the scope of this book, which is basically about parenting children between 0-12 years of age, abstinence-only sex education is what I recommend and shall be discussing.

From 0-2 years, let your child be familiar with his or her body parts. Also, ensure that you name the body parts by their proper names, don't use pet names like your parents did please, that was the analogue age, remember? Masking the real names of genitals or body parts may give your child the impression that they are shrouded in secrecy and that it is some sort of taboo to call them by their real names. Let your child know that strangers are not allowed to touch their privates and they should let you know if anyone at all touches their genitals or other sensitive body parts. Also, let your child know that it is okay to touch his or her genitals. It is self-exploratory and very normal. Don't shout or scream when you see them playing with their genitals or fondling it casually. They're simply getting used to their genitals and the feelings they produce. However, discourage them from doing so often or in public.

At age 3-6, your child is now familiar with the difference between male and female. Let him or her know the body parts of the opposite sex at this point. Emphasize that no stranger should touch their privates and they should alert you if there is any such case. Likewise, let him or her know that other people's privates are also out of bounds. Let your kid know that while it is okay to touch the genitals occasionally, he or she should only do so in private and not in public. Teach your child about good and bad touch at this stage. Let him or her know that good touch is a casual, friendly touch but bad touch is an intimate and lingering touch on any part of the body. Also teach your kid to tell anyone giving them a bad touch to stop and that he or she should leave the place immediately and report to a parent or teacher.

At age 7-9, your child may have started noticing changes in his or her body. Talk to him or her about puberty and the body changes expected at this stage. Talk about how semen is produced, about menstruation, sanitary towels, wet dreams, etc. Also, begin to talk about sexual intercourse and the need to be chaste. You can make use of picture books and charts to further illustrate what you're teaching.

At age 10-12, begin to go more in depth with your child. Talk about personal hygiene that is more important now as a result of puberty. Tell him or her that people attain puberty at different rates and whatever growth rate he or she has, is normal. At this age, children often worry about whether they're "normal" — especially regarding penis and breast size. You need to reassure your child. You might want to share your own experiences so your child will know that it is normal and that you have been through that phase also. Talk more about sexual intercourse at this stage. Teach your child not to discuss sex with strangers or 'sext' with strangers. Let your child know the dangers of sharing nude pictures with strangers online. Let him or her know the dangers of pornography.

By the way, don't talk only about the repercussions of sex, talk also about the enjoyment, let your child know it is pleasurable but only allowed for married couples. Keep reinforcing the things you've been teaching.

Oops! Not so bad, is it? Even if it is, it is still your duty to ensure you're the go-to person for your child when it comes to sexuality issues. Even if they see anything online, our children should be able to double-check with us as parents.

Before we round off on this juicy sex talk, let's have some more tips on sexually educating our children.

- When your child asks questions about sex or sexuality, ask what he or she already knows. Most of the time, they have heard something outside and want to confirm.

- Confirm what they already know, if true.

- Correct any misconceptions, if any.

- Take your time to explain as deeply as possible and appropriate.

- Never dismiss your child's sexual questions.

- Never laugh at your child's questions or scold them for it.

- Seize teachable opportunities to discuss sex. Scenes from movies and real life occurrences can be used to pass across salient messages.

- Give accurate and honest answers. When you don't have the answers, let your child know and promise to find out. Don't forget to fulfill your promise.

- Protect your child from lewd music and movies. Know the age-appropriate music and movies for your child and be firm about not letting them view unsuitable content.

Explain to them why they're not allowed to watch such content at this stage.

- Don't scare your child away from sex by stigmatizing it. Trust me, it's counterproductive. Lay the facts bare and guide him or her appropriately.

At the end of the day, our children will still have to make their choices. But we would be confident that we've equipped them to make the right decisions.

CHAPTER NINE
SHOW THE TALK!

"Well done is better than well said."
-Benjamin Franklin

Ireti's mother smiled as she chatted with her friend on the phone. Later, she started giggling. "Mum," Ireti called. Her mother did not answer. "Mum, I think...," she started. "Shut up! I told you to stop disturbing me when I'm on the phone. When will you learn?" her mother snapped at her. Seven-year-old Ireti sat down quietly and continued watching the TV. Five minutes later – "Oh my God! Ireti, can't you smell the beans burning? What are you useful for in this house? It's only TV you know how to watch."

Dad: Efe, go to your room, you're not allowed to watch violent movies. You're still nine years old. These movies are not appropriate for your age. When you become an adult, then you can watch them, okay? Now, run along!

Efe: (thinking to himself) Oh, so now I'm not old enough to watch violent movies? What about the ones I watch every other day in this house; you punching mum and she throwing stuff at you? The only thing missing in your own movies is a gun.

Emeka and his dad are in the living room, having a dancing competition. "Dad, I can dance 'shaku shaku' better than you," Emeka said, grinning. "For where? I will show you I won dancing competitions for my school in my days," said Emeka's dad, sweating and panting as he was trying to keep up with the beats of one of the trendiest singles in town, while also singing along rapturously. The lyrics? Here you go: "When I get hold of you, I will lay your back on the bed and give it to you hard. Can you see my cassava? It's bigger than your boyfriend's own."

Teacher: Daniel! I'm going to ask you for the last time, where did you get the video you were watching? (She had caught him and a couple of friends watching a porn video on his tablet during break time.)

Daniel: Ma, I erm erm…

Teacher: Answer me! You think I'm joking here, right?

Daniel: I erm copied it erm from erm my mummy's laptop.

FYI, Daniel is just eight years old.

(A woman in her living room, talking to her children)

Mother: As I was saying, don't ever lie. Always say the truth even if you're going to be punished, okay?

Children: Okay, Mummy.

Mother: Good. As children of God, we ought not to lie. Anyone who lies is a child of the devil… (phone rings and mother picks her call). "Hello, how are you, Mama Bola? Okay… you're on your way to my house? Ah, I'm not at home. I'm out of town. Yes. I've been out of town for one week now. I will be back next week. I'll call you when I'm back, okay? Alright, bye." (Faces children) Ehn ehn, my children, as I was saying, all liars have a space in hell fire…

Now, before you laugh or smirk, you need to think deeply and ask yourself if you don't fall into any of these categories. I mean it, think deeply. It is not enough to lay down rules and regulations and have systems in place; you need to model what you preach. Research has shown that children do what they see us do, not what we tell them to do. No matter how many times we tell them to do something or behave in a particular way, if our lifestyle is contrary to what we tell them to do, they won't do it. If you tell your children not to lie but they see you lie on the phone regularly, they'll just laugh at you behind your back and they will lie, don't be fooled.

So, how can we be good examples as parents? How can we walk our talk? First, we need to be open and sincere. Let your sincerity show in all you do and say. Be an open book; let your child be able to read you. Don't be deceived, your child knows when you pretend. There's no way you'll hide your real self and expect your child to be open with you. Once your child knows you're two-faced, he or she will never trust you, and it will be a license for that child to be double-faced also.

Another way we can be good models of what we preach to our children in this WiFi age is to limit our screen time. Some women practically live on social media. They want to catch up on the latest gist as well as do 'pepper-dem-gang'. They get their daily dose of self-esteem from the likes, comments, shares and follows they get on social media. They will fall sick if they're unable to go online in a day. They neglect all house chores and child care once they have their phone with them. So, in order not to get disturbed, they engage their children with another device. Yet, they do a 360° and tell their children to limit screen time and even set rules. Really? Who are they deceiving?

Men are also not exempt from this scourge. Some men are always playing games on their phones or tablets. The only time they're at home is in the evenings and weekends and a chunk of that time is spent playing games and watching movies on their phones. They stay late into the night to watch movies, yet emphasize the importance of sleep and set bed time for their children. If you belong to this class, remember that what you're doing is louder than what you're saying. Now, I know some of us work and read on our phones, I do also. What I do is let my children know that I am working and not binging. When you're transparent, your children will believe you and take you seriously.

Some of us are good lecturers. We know how to lecture our children on good conduct. We tell them not to sing songs with vulgar lyrics. We scold them when they even hum the songs. We ban them from watching music channels on TV, but guess what? We sing the songs ourselves! We know all the lyrics and sing along when the music plays on the radio in our cars. Some of us even buy those CDs and play them in our cars. What do we think we have for children? Dummies? They observe and take in more than you think they do. And this has nothing to do with age. A couple noticed their 11-month-old occasionally wriggling his hips in a very sexual way. At first, they thought it was his new style of play. It later dawned on them that the poor boy was mimicking their lovemaking style. They make love in front of the boy! They thought he was just a baby. Baby indeed!

If you watch x-rated movies with or in front of your children, I have one word for you: You need help fast! Okay, that was four words but the point is clear, right? As bizarre as this may sound, some parents do it. They watch porn in front of their kids. They leave the CDs carelessly in the house. They leave the videos carelessly on their devices. Before you shake your head and walk away, if you watch movies rated 16 or 18 in front of your ten-year-old or any age below the stipulated age, you belong to this gang. There's a reason these movies are suitable for certain ages and this isn't just about sex or violence. There are stuffs our children can't process at a certain age and if they're exposed to them at that age, they can cause trauma for them or even distract them from their studies because they keep trying to process them and make meaning out of them. It is your duty to make life as easy as possible for your child, not complicate it.

Some of us are fond of taking our kids to see movies rated for ages beyond their age grade just because the movies are trending or we have nowhere to put them. This is very wrong. The producers of these movies consult with child psychologists and other experts to determine the suitable audience. Respect that! It is not for their benefit, it is for yours. They have done their part, do yours! Think about it: you'll be helping them make money at the detriment of the future of your child. If the doctor prescribes one tablet for your sick child, will you give him or her two tablets just so it can work fast? I didn't think so! But that is exactly what you do when you expose your children to content beyond their age grade. And if you're a cinema owner or a staff and you allow children below the stipulated age to see a movie because you want to make more money, well done! You're likened to a pharmacist who increases the dosage for a sick child so he or she can sell more medicine. If a pharmacist does that for you, won't you sue? Don't forget, the things you enable today will come back and haunt you tomorrow. That child you're allowing to watch unsuitable movies may be your child's best friend tomorrow, he or she may be that stranger your child is secretly chatting with on the internet and he or she may be the one to marry your child many years down the line. What goes around…

To be great models as parents, we need a measure of vulnerability. Yes, I know that we were brought up by parents who were demi-gods and could do no wrong. That's why we became so bitter and angry at life when our parents separated and/or divorced. Our picture perfect parents were suddenly fallible and had real flaws and struggles which we were not aware of, because they painted a certain picture of perfection for us. That was in the analogue age, Darling Parent! In this WiFi era, your child sees more than he or she lets on even if they don't talk. You need to let him or her know you also struggle with these rules you're setting and that you can be corrected when wrong.

Generally speaking, people are freer with someone who's vulnerable and admits to being imperfect than someone who claims to have it all together all the time. When you're vulnerable, you make people feel comfortable around you, they tend to open up to you better because they believe you can relate with their struggles and you won't judge them. We should be the same with our children. Now, that's not to say we shouldn't be that solid backbone every child needs. We need to project a measure of dependability to be great parents but we should also endeavor to create that much-needed balance.

Consistency is non-negotiable if your aim is to be a good example to your child. Giving one rule today and changing it tomorrow will not generate respect from your child. They'll simply not take you seriously. Telling them it's wrong to lie and showing them it's okay to lie in certain instances is inconsistency. You condemn government officials for taking bribes, yet make phone calls in front of your child to ask for kickbacks from potential clients at your office, and you expect your child to believe you hate corruption? Think again! You say bedtime is 9pm but you allow your child stay up till 11pm sometimes? That's inconsistency!

Lastly, to be a good role model, you need to confide in your child. It's a law of nature; people are likely to confide in those who confide in them. If you want your child to talk to you when he's having his first crush or when a boy is sending her love notes and she's having butterflies in her stomach, then you need to model it. Tell them stuff you would normally not tell them; things that are considered confidential. Tell them your fears about your promotion; tell them the excitement you'll feel when you buy that new car; tell them how you're struggling to raise their fees; ask for their advice even. When you do this, you encourage them to follow suit. They see you as an ally, someone they share a special bond with, someone they shouldn't hide things from.

Yes, I know it is not easy being a role model when you're still struggling with some of these vices yourself, but no one said parenting is easy. It is a huge responsibility to raise a child and if you're fortunate to be a parent, please do all you can to bring up that child well, especially in this WiFi age. No one is saying you have to be perfect but you have to do your best. Parenting takes work. You're the first person your child knows in life and he or she will always be looking up to you. Be sure not to disappoint.

EPILOGUE
BRIDGING THE GAP

Yes, I know I've teased us about being the analogue generation and I've given us many reasons to be WiFi-compliant all through this book. However, being analogue has its benefits. Let's take the Nokia phone for example. Yes, the famous 3310. Even though it is no longer fashionable in the WiFi age, it stands for qualities like ruggedness and durability. Many brands like the Blackberry and the iPhone actually came on board to beat the Nokia standard. If Nokia had no standard, there would have been nothing to beat. It's the same with us. Even though most of the parenting methods we grew up to know are archaic now, it still doesn't undermine the parenting standard set by our parents. It is our duty to pass over the values and principles of the analogue era into the WiFi age. It is our duty to be the bridge.

We may not sit our children down under the almond tree to tell them tales by moonlight, but we can teach them the lessons we learnt from those stories. We may not gather in the living room to watch Network News together, but we can teach them the importance of being aware of situations and happenings in the country and around the world. We may not trek miles to the local market together but we can teach them the art of bargaining and negotiation our mothers taught us. We may not play oldies on the record players our fathers played them on but we can give them a glimpse of what good music should sound like and how different it is from the noise that is obtainable now.

We may not cook with firewood anymore but we can teach them that there's joy in putting effort into an activity that gives you pleasure. We may not wash clothes with our hands anymore but we can teach them how to do it so they will be able to survive anywhere they find themselves. We may not take them to the farm but we can teach them the principles of sowing and reaping. We may not have the communal parties and traditions anymore but we can teach them to value any community they find themselves.

Yes, we may have a microwave in the kitchen now but we can teach them that some things in life don't get microwaved; you need to wait for it to thaw. We may have a car to go anywhere we want but we must teach them the benefits of long walks and the need to respect those who can't afford the luxury. We may have access to social media, where anonymity makes people talk to others disrespectfully but we must teach them to respect everyone even if they cannot see them.

We may celebrate other people's achievements on social media and appreciate the rave to fast track our lives but we must remind our children that the good things in life take time, hard work and diligence. We might appreciate the glitz and glamour of social media but we must teach our kids not to compare themselves with others and stay on their lanes. We may 'feel among' and live in the moment but we must not forget our analogue and evergreen values and the need for us to be the bridge.

REFERENCES

Jukes et al. (2010), Understanding the Digital Generation: Teaching and Learning in the New Digital Landscape, Hawker Brownlow

New Zealand on Air, & Broadcasting Standards Authority. (2015). *Children's Media Use Study: How our children engage with media today*. Retrieved from https://bsa.govt.nz/images/assets/Research/Childrens_Media_Report_2015_FINAL_for_publishing_2.pdf

Unicef, 2017, Children in a Digital World. Retrieved from https://www.unicef.org/bulgaria/media/

https://www.ofcom.org.uk/research-and-data/media-literacy-research/childrens/children-and-parents-media-use-and-attitudes-report-2018
https://vitalrecord.tamhsc.edu/decreasing-age-puberty/

https://en.wikipedia.org/wiki/History_of_YouTube

https://www.engadget.com/2016/11/10/the-history-of-youtube

https://mashable.com/youtubehistory

https://www.commonsensemedia.org/

https://mashable.com/2013/10/28/children-under-2-mobile-media-study/

https://www.aap.org/en-us/about-the-aap/aap-press-room/Pages/American-Academy-of-Pediatrics-Supports-Childhood-Sleep-Guidelines.aspx

https://www.nhs.uk/news/neurology/lack-of-sleep-may-disrupt-development-of-a-childs-brain/

https://www.parents.com/health/healthy-happy-kids/the-7-reasons-your-kid-needs-sleep/

www.ingramcontent.com/pod-product-compliance
Lightning Source LLC
Chambersburg PA
CBHW030322160726
47992CB00005B/2117